Understanding William Golding's Lor

- **A complete GCSE Study Guide for Summer 2015 & 2016 Exams.**

By Gavin Smithers

Another one of **Gavin's Guides** – study books packed with insight. They aim to help you raise your grade!

Understanding William Golding's Lord of the Flies is a complete study guide and has been written especially for students and teachers who are preparing for GCSE in Summer 2015 and 2016.

Series Editor: Gill Chilton

The complete text of Lord of the Flies (Faber & Faber) is widely available, including on Amazon. You will need a copy of this text, in paperback or as an e-book, to use alongside this Study Guide.

Let's get started

William Golding's novel "Lord of the Flies" has been a favourite text for GCSE for many years, for several reasons. It is not a long novel (it has twelve chapters), and its language is quite straightforward. It has a range of interesting themes, which makes it easy to formulate exam questions based on the text.

If you've bought this book because "Lord of the Flies" is part of what you have to study for GCSE English, then, in my opinion, you've taken another step towards doing well in your exam.

This book has been written specifically to assist GCSE candidates who are taking the AQA, OCR and WJEC exams in 2015.

It is also excellent to have it at hand early in your studies. If you are a current Year 10 student, your GCSEs won't be until summer 2016. But I believe this Study Guide can also help you now, during the first year of your course.

"Lord of the Flies" was published in 1954. Sixty or so years later, it still has some interesting questions to ask about how the world can be kept safe, in a nuclear age.

It explores what society would be like if we had no rules of behaviour to contain violence and cruelty. It asks us to think about the extent to which the grown-up world and the world of the school playground are really the same; we can see conflict in both.

The book presents a view that all people, all over the world, have some drives which can be damaging if we have no means of controlling them. And it questions the assumption that

Britain, and its people, are somehow better, or more civilised, than people from other parts of the world.

With regard to Britain (and indeed to any country, anywhere) this is always relevant; how do we treat people who depend on us, and how do we expect our citizens to behave? Do we end up with the leaders we deserve? Do we tend to think of our own nation, or race, as better than others? If we do, how do we justify that, and are we right to?

You won't find the characters in the story discussing these issues; such questions don't even occur to the boys on the island. What is clever about the novel is that, while it works as a story about some boys stranded on a tropical island in the Pacific Ocean, it is not just a boys' adventure story.

It has a secondary or **allegorical meaning;** we won't understand the novel properly unless we get to grips with this (hidden) aspect of it.

Of course, this guide will help you with that. In addition to covering plot and characters, I also explain key themes - so you'll have a head start to impressing your exam marker with your understanding and ability to show what you know.

So why a Gavin's Guide? It is likely you have discovered that there are a fair few study guides on this text already- you or your class-mates may already have some of them. And many of them are useful reference points for summaries of the plot and the characters.

But few, if any, explain or analyse in as much detail as this guide does how Golding manages and organises our response as we read.

Understanding this- and being able to show the examiner that you do- will mean that you will be more able to achieve a good grade.

It is **the depth of your understanding** which makes the difference; and that's what this guide will give you.

I am a private tutor in Broadway, Worcestershire, and this book was initially written for my English Literature students, to help them achieve good grades and an understanding of what this clever, articulate writer wanted to say. Now, whether you prefer it as a paperback or an e-book, I hope it will help you too.

What this short guide can do

This guide will help you understand clearly what Golding wanted to say when he wrote "Lord of the Flies".

You will find **a detailed analysis**, both of the plot, **chapter by chapter**, and of the individual **characters**. You don't have to read the whole guide in one go; it will work as a **reference** and revision guide, especially if you need to remind yourself of **what happens when**.

Look for key insights and important points; I've put them in **bold type**, when I think there is **something you really need to take in.**

However, at GCSE level you can't get a really good grade just by knowing what happens in a book. You need to be able to **show you understand the "why" and "how"** of the ways in which authors create their texts.

I believe that we must concentrate on developing a very clear sense of what the novel is about. The meaning is more than the story; it's more than the characters; it's more than the key or recurring themes. Being aware of each of those strands will, however, help to lead us to the meaning,

The acid test of great literature is that it makes us think about something for the first time, or it makes us think about something familiar in a new way.

Being aware of our thoughts, when we read, will help us to define the meaning and the message which lies behind the story and the words on the page. And pinning down the meaning and the message will make us appreciate more the skill with which Golding has written it.

As with many novelists, Golding's art and skill depends on links, connections and cross-references throughout the story he tells us. We may not be conscious of them, especially on a first reading- I highlight those links.

This guide is not a substitute for a close reading of the novel. I suggest you read all of Golding's tale **before you start using this guide,** for two reasons.

1. Independent reading of your own will start to *help you develop your own response to what you read*; this guide will show you why you respond as you do. It's a skill you can then apply to all the texts you have to study for this GCSE.

2. I give away the plot, and do so right at the start of this Study Guide. Anyone who reads this guide before reading the novel will lose their appreciation of the dramatic tensions in the novel, because **you will know what happens** before you've read it. So you need to read the text first *to keep in the dramatic tension*. These tensions among the main characters lead to a tense, gripping climax in the last two chapters; Golding handles it brilliantly.

So I recommend that you read the novel; then read this guide; then read the novel again. You will find yourself referring back to the novel, too, when you read my chapter by chapter analysis.

Understanding what is in, and behind, the text is the first task. But that counts for little, unless we can also **write a really good essay**. I want to help you with that too!

The final part of this guide gives you three essay questions and answers. When you read them, you will see that planning your answer, and making a list of the material you'll be including, gives you a really solid structure. It should also take away any temptation you feel to carry on writing after you've dealt with all of the stuff you need to include!

Wasting time by writing too much of the wrong stuff- usually, because of the temptation, under the time pressure of an exam, to start writing without making a plan first- is the easiest way to do worse than you should. I don't want that to happen to you!

What's in this guide will spark your own ideas. Take them back to your lessons, and have some interesting discussions there. Ask your teacher to explain anything which puzzles you; when you've done that, if there's something you still don't understand, you can e-mail me at grnsmithers@hotmail.co.uk.

Getting to grips with the key ideas of this book

"Lord of the Flies" was published in 1954, and it was William Golding's first novel.

It is unusual, in its complete exclusion of any female characters (unless you count the sow, which is hunted and killed with elaborate cruelty). It is notable, too, that, apart from the naval officer who has a walk-on part at the end of the novel, none of the characters is old enough even to be a teenager (the boys' ages range from six to twelve).

Golding gains more than he loses by adopting this pre-teen perspective. In particular, it enables him to populate the world of the desert island with childish- but very real- objects of fear. This bundle of irrational fears coalesces into the idea of the beast- a term which is applied at various points to various objects of terror, and which has an interesting range of composite meanings.

He chooses to drop a large group of schoolboys on to the uninhabited island so that he can explore the difference between a social system governed by institutional rules (like a school) and a so-called society where there are no rules, because there are no adults to apply or impose them.

It is a fairly short step from the rules which govern a school to the laws which govern our prison and justice system, or to the framework of international law which constrains the behaviour of whole nations. In each case, we may take the rules for granted, or forget the point of having them. Golding's argument seems to be that rules are necessary in order to protect the weak, and avoid anarchy. We may (complacently) think that people are basically well behaved, cooperative and civilised. Golding shows us a different side of human nature- one where being made to adhere to rules suppresses vicious cruelty, casual violence, savagery and beastliness. How far has mankind evolved from its animalistic ancestry? Perhaps, Golding suggests, not as far as we would like to think.

As you read the book, you may question the significance of there only being boys, or perhaps wonder whether a very different series of events would have unfolded if there had been boys and girls, or even only girls. All these are valid trains of thought. However, I don't think Golding failed to introduce girls because of any effect it may have had on the outcome.

If Jack had been Jade could she have been the hunter? Of course she could!

In my view, Golding did not include girls because he was writing about what he knew (he had been a teacher in a boys' school) and he was interested in how mankind behave (that is society, not just men) and didn't want his message diluted by other issues, such as sexism or feminism or how, during the growing up years of around 12, boys and girls may act with shyness around each other.

One of the most successful aspects of this novel is the way in which the narrative point of view narrows, as Ralph loses his allies and supporters, so that his isolation and his apparently hopeless attempts to escape being hunted to death in the final chapter are very memorable.

For most of the novel, however, we are observing a power struggle between Ralph and Jack, to determine who is the chief. We are reading an extended exploration of the issue of leadership. Leaders can be good or bad, and so can those who consent to be led. It is difficult to avoid the feeling that the whole story is allegorical, that is to say it has a sustained, parallel meaning, as well as functioning as a novel.

Could it be that Golding is debating how global peace can be secured in a world where the Second World War has been brought to an end only by dropping an atomic bomb on Japan just nine years earlier? If this is the real motive for rewriting the story concept of some boys stranded on a remote island, then our interest in the plot and the characters is really just a means to an end.

Golding has filled his tale with doubt and suspense because he thinks that, in the 1950s, with two nuclear powers (the USA and the USSR) juggling with an uneasy truce, our need for a peaceful world is also in doubt. Like the fragile peace on the island between Ralph and Jack, world peace hangs by a delicate thread. Just like Jack, a superpower could lose its restraint and become an aggressor; if that were allowed to happen, what would the consequences be?

Rather as Shakespeare cannot avoid making Juliet (in "Romeo and Juliet") think and talk in ways which are older than her official age of thirteen, so Ralph, Piggy and Jack often seem older than twelve.

Golding has to do this because he is writing for an older (adult) readership; generally books that have lead characters aged 12 and younger are books written for children to read. But Golding is a serious, adult author and he went on to win the Nobel Prize for Literature in 1983.

That award came with the comment that Golding's novels "illuminate the human condition in the world of today"- they have something to say to us about the world we live in; and that he combines "realistic narrative"- creating stories we find convincing and characters who seem real- with "the universality of myth"- something which is timeless and always relevant, because it deals with basic emotions like fear, anger, and the need to reach out to other people.

If Golding had denied himself the room to develop, in his characters, including characters in this young age group, an emotional awareness which belongs more properly to an older age group, he would have written a flatter and less interesting novel.

This is not to say that "Lord of the Flies" is a timeless or perfect work of art; it is not. *Some of the language and the attitudes, as well as some aspects of the narrative style, are dated or one-dimensional or jarring.* I will pay attention to these faults later in this guide.

It is, however, **a very original novel**, because it succeeds in weaving together its own drama with timeless philosophical questions about leadership, society, government and morality.

And, in Piggy, it leaves us with a memorable character; a whining, unathletic, myopic, asthmatic, fat anti-hero, whose courage and insight live on long after we have forgotten Ralph, Jack and the others.

More than just a story:

Psychology theories and how they work on a desert island

In the same year that Golding's novel appeared, the American psychologist Abraham Maslow published a book called "Motivation and Personality", which developed ideas he had first publicised in 1943.

Maslow's theory is generally understood to argue that human beings have a scale or hierarchy of needs; only fulfilling or satisfying the needs which arise at each stage or level allows humanity- or the individual- to advance to the next one. It is only rare and exceptional people who can see beyond their immediate unsatisfied need, and strive, also, for a better society.

Maslow's work describes the way individual human minds work, but perhaps we can apply it to nations, too, in the 1950s.

After a World War from 1939-1945, there was now the threat of nuclear war. Whole nations, and the people who make them up, will have been frightened of each other, and of the new capacity for violence. How might they be tempted to respond to that threat, and how should they deal with those fears? Can we still be polite and friendly with countries which (like Roger and the rock he drops on Piggy) have their hands on the button which will send nuclear missiles in our direction?

The most basic need is for physical survival- it will naturally predominate over everything else, and it requires food, shelter and clothing. Once these needs are met, the human psyche turns to the need for safety- especially in children.

The next need, after that, is a social one- the need to belong to or identify with a group (or family, or tribe). It is so strong that it can override the need for safety. The need to belong and be accepted can drive our behaviour. Think of how all the boys desert Ralph to join Jack's tribe- only Piggy, Simon, Sam and Eric, and some "littluns" are left. Think of the fan clubs football teams and popular bands attract.

Beyond this stage, Maslow finds that people have a drive for (self-) esteem and (self-) respect. The "lower" category is the need for respect from other people (which Jack constantly seeks as a hunter, and thinks he is entitled to, as a head boy and as head chorister) - a need for recognition, status and attention. The "higher" form is to do with being able to live with ourselves; feeling that we are capable and competent to do what is expected of us, or what we ourselves expect, because of our own standards of behaviour. It shows through being self-confident, independent-minded, strong and resilient.

We see Jack struggling to cope with his sense of guilt over the failure of the boys' society (and the deaths of Simon and Piggy), after he was chosen to lead it. Maslow pointed out that these levels of needs can overlap; they are interrelated. Although Ralph is self-denying and Jack is self-indulgent, there is an area of overlap; Ralph would like to hunt, because it is exciting, and Jack would like the responsibility of being chief. It is clear, though, that Jack is lower and Ralph is higher, when we judge them on Maslow's criteria; and that is the right way to look at them.

The highest need, Maslow finds, is one which applies only to adults, not children- the longer- term project of reaching our individual potential, or "self-actualization". It is only at this stage of our development that we can be effective at improving the wider world we live in.

We certainly recognise (as Ralph does, to his own frustration) that it is unrealistic to expect children to behave with the judgment of adults, when they have none of an adult's experience and perspective.

Additional research has found- unsurprisingly- that, for children, the basic physical needs are more dominant, while the end of childhood is the point at which the needs to belong and for esteem begin to emerge. This helps us to see the distinction between Golding's "littluns" and "biguns".

Other psychologists of this era were interested in "attachment theory" (a term coined by John Bowlby). Piggy's parents are dead; Ralph has no mother. Golding seems to be interested in what happens to displaced children (of whom there were very many during the Second World War). If you have no family with you (and no one on the island does), what kind of relationships do you form? What is the function of the tribe? Do you make bad decisions, just for the sake of belonging to something? How does it feel to be outside, or excluded from the tribe? Look at the last two chapters of the novel for the answers to these questions!

Some of the theories of a psychologist from the generation before Maslow also influence critical analysis of Golding- that is Sigmund Freud (1856-1939). Freud developed the terms "id", "ego" and "superego".

The "id" (perhaps "the thing"- or even the beast!) is the drive to be impulsive; it demands that we gratify the momentary impulse, and Jack's obsession with hunting is this sort of drive.

The "ego" is a more reflective and socially responsible part of us; it restrains us in our selfish drives, by considering the effect of gratifying our own wishes, and trying to be pragmatic and realistic, not just selfish. This strikes a chord with us on the occasions where Ralph says he would like to experience the excitement of hunting, but he has to build shelters and manage fire duties instead.

The "superego" is the power external influences have over our behaviour- the restraining influences of the messages we receive from our parents, role models, authority figures and our cultural norms. This accounts for the taboo which prevents Roger from throwing stones at Henry to hit him; by Chapter 11, he throws stones much closer to Ralph's head, and there is not much doubt he intends the rock to hit Piggy. It explains why Piggy is constantly asking "what will the grown-ups say/think?" if and when they hear what is going on.

Golding shows us that, in any group, these restraining forces wear off sooner or later. He is asking us to consider what the balance between the ego and the superego has on social coherence; and what we should do about the id.

The conflict between thinking and feeling

There is a striking scene at the end of Chapter 5, where Jack is becoming more powerful, and Simon and Piggy have to cajole Ralph to carry on leading the boys. They wish their adult relatives were on hand, because then things would be smoother and safe. Ralph keeps coming up against the same problem – the younger boys have nightmares, and because they are disturbed and emotionally exhausted they cannot do the things they really need to do (build shelters, and keep a large fire going, so that any passing ship can rescue them).

However much Ralph, or anyone, tells the younger boys that there is no monster in the forest, they will still believe there is. There may be no evidence for it, but the evidence of their own imaginations is all they need. By allowing the risk of the existence of a "beast" to creep into their thoughts, they are fearful all the time, which stops them from doing what needs to be done.

Piggy explains this, not in terms of a monster, but in terms of Jack (in fact, it's a useful comparison!). Piggy says that, when you hate and fear something or someone, you can't get it/them out of your thoughts. Piggy has good reason to fear Jack, and to worry that Jack will hurt him. The boys on the island fear a monster they have never actually seen, but their thoughts about it give it the same power over them as if it were real.

From Chapter 6 onwards, there are physical objects which some boys think *are* a monster- either the dead parachutist, or Simon, or the wild boar. But, in Chapter 5, the fear is that they are sharing the island with a sea-monster or a sea-snake or a ghost.

In the end, even Jack- who has seen more of the island than anyone else- has to give up trying to persuade the others that there is no beast (only Simon does not believe in it, ever). Jack ends up fuelling the fear and the myth, by leaving part of the pig he kills as a peace offering to it. So the boys, as a group, try to appease an imagined monster they have no proper reason to believe is real.

They only believe in it at all because of what some of them *think they have seen*. But that is enough for the monster to take on a life of its own, *while Golding is telling us is that the really frightening thing is the monster within-* **the potential in us, as people and as gangs of people, to be violent to others, for no good reason except that we are afraid of them**.

Allowing the feeling of fear to dictate what we do (or, in the novel's terms, which parts of the island we can visit, and which are no go areas) *just grinds us down*, when, often, there is not even anything we should be afraid of. <u>Irrational feelings drive away rational, reasoned thoughts; and eventually we forget how to think rationally.</u>

Golding was a school-teacher, so he understood that one purpose of education is to teach us how to think rationally- how to weigh up evidence and make sensible decisions, based on what we know, rather than just what we feel.

The prominent American psychologist Albert Ellis argued that irrational thinking (nightmares about the beast) is damaging, and needs to be treated by thinking rationally, in order to contain distress. Ralph's wellbeing hangs by a thread, as his responses to stressful events on the island become less rational, from the start of Chapter 5 onwards.

Savages under the skin

When we analyse "Lord of the Flies" in terms of the psychology it explores, we are helped in our search for its meaning. By putting a group of children (as opposed to adults) into an "uncivilised" environment, Golding can explore the potential for regression; the idea that the boys are British, and therefore, by definition, cannot be savage, turns out to be nonsense.

One convincing interpretation of the novel is that, for Golding, who had fought in the Second World War, the potential for cruelty and dehumanising behaviour is universal; so is the craving for safety.

How, then, can we reconcile personal (and national) needs for safety with others' personal (and national) needs for safety? How can we ensure that, under the stress of conflicts in leadership or fear, we avoid the anarchy of the irrational, or of more world wars? How do we contain sadism (Emperor Hirohito of Japan, during World War 2, and Roger); repression and megalomania (Stalin/Hitler and Jack); and how do we treat the post-traumatic condition of the boys who have survived seeing others killed- in particular, Ralph, who feels he failed to achieve, as leader, what should have been possible?

So, if these are the questions that this novel asks … where are the answers? Unsatisfyingly perhaps, Golding does not tell us what he thinks! So the answers must come from our personal responses and beliefs. As an exam candidate however, that does have the benefit that you cannot be wrong: your argument, if it is made rationally, is always right!

Timeline and narrative techniques

In one sense, the plot of the novel is limited in its range- a group of boys land on a desert island; three die (the boy with the facial birthmark, Simon and Piggy); the rest are rescued.

This simplified summary, though, does not account for the dramatic tension. Particularly in the last quarter of the book, Golding has us turning those pages. His control of pace is skilled. He also creates some depth in his main characters. We feel we know how Piggy, Ralph and Simon think- we are inside their minds. We are appalled witnesses, too, of the violent and hateful instincts of Jack and Roger, which surely need to be reined in.

The pace of the story; where our sympathies lie; the balance between action and drama, and between the thoughts and feelings of the characters- these are all aspects of the narrative which deserve our attention, because analysing them reveals the nature of Golding's skill.

The novel is in twelve chapters. Chapter 1 is the longest, followed by chapters 8, 12 (the last one), and 5. Each chapter has a title; this is unusual in adult fiction.

The wording of the chapter titles points us to important elements of the story- the shell, fire, the beast, darkness, death, the glasses, hunters. It is a child-like device that is not strictly necessary for older readers. However, the words the chapter titles highlight do imply that we should be focussing on the symbolic, dark and dangerous elements of the plot.

The influence of "The Coral Island"

"The Coral Island" is the name of a famous 19th century novel. The phrase, "The Coral Island" is mentioned twice in Golding's novel; once, at the end (by the rescuing naval officer) and once near the start of Chapter 2. Its importance to Golding extends to the fact that the original novel's three main characters are called Jack, Ralph and Peterkin. Adopting the names Ralph and Jack, and a name beginning with P (Piggy) for the third boy, cannot be just a coincidence.

"The Coral Island" appeared in 1857 (almost exactly a century before "Lord of the Flies"); it was written by RM Ballantyne, a British (Scottish) author. It relates the adventures of three boys who are shipwrecked; they build a shelter, explore, hunt pigs and live in a state of continual contentment and harmony. The dialogue is assembled so that bits of botany and natural history are included. The eighteenth and nineteenth centuries saw British sailors and explorers colonising exotic places like this, all over the world, and claiming them as British possessions.

Two groups of cannibals land on the island and fight a battle, which the boys get involved in. Ralph is abducted by pirates, which enables Ballantyne to go out of his way to praise the dangerous work of evangelists from the London Missionary Society, and depict the savagery and cruel superstitions of the uncivilised South Pacific native islanders.

When Piggy's brains are dashed out on the rock, Golding may be revisiting Ballantyne's style of narrative, which barely stops for breath, however violently a character dies.

Ballantyne presents the idea that converting primitive savages to Christianity is vital, in order to prevent cannibalism, evil superstitions (such as, when a king dies, his wives must be strangled too) and all manner of cruelty. He also presents the concept (we cannot be sure whether any irony is intended) that young English men are brave, enterprising, moral and culturally superior in every way. In "The Coral Island", there is nothing disturbing in the way the pigs are hunted, and the boys never fight amongst themselves.

Ballantyne's story is fast-paced and quite exciting in its way. Golding revisits it because he wants to dissect what lies under the surface of an English education and how we British see ourselves in relation to the rest of the world. The naval officer assumes that the boys have behaved with decency and dignity, as British boys should- but this Ralph and this Jack and this Peterkin (Piggy) are much more complex than the characters they are modelled on, and their conflicts do not begin with the external violence of cannibals or pirates.

They arise from how easy they find it to abandon British rules of decent behaviour when there are no adults to punish the rule-breakers (remember how keen Jack was on rules, as a British convention, in Chapter 1).

Detailed analysis of the plot

Chapter 1

The first chapter of any novel has to do two things; set the scene in an accurate way, so that the reader has a true idea of what to expect, and create enough questions and curiosity in our mind to make us read on.

Golding sets the scene, introducing the key elements of the scenery on the island, and the key characters, in their proper order- Ralph, then Piggy, then Jack (and then, among others, Simon and Roger). He arouses our curiosity by withholding the boys' names to begin with.

Note how much he tells us about them. **Piggy** is fat and asthmatic; he is undignified, and **grunts a lot (like a pig)**; he is **friendly and intelligent**; and he tries to attach himself to Ralph. He would like to be the leader himself (that is why he is slow to put his hand up in support of Ralph) but he understands that he does not have the charisma that job demands.

Jack is presented to us carefully. His choir are oddly dressed, in black (black caps, black cloaks, like blackbirds) and he **makes violent gestures with a knife**. He talks in a strange public school language. He assumes that he should be the leader, because he leads the choir, has a golden cap badge, can sing high notes, and is a head boy; he thinks, with what Golding terms simple arrogance, that he should automatically be chosen.

Golding tells us, in the narrative, that Jack is the most obvious leader, because of his self-confidence and his offhand authority. But this is not the enclosed and high-powered world of the public school. Jack is remarkably unsympathetic to Simon's fainting or fits, and he is rude to Piggy.

Moreover, he has neither Ralph's attractiveness, mildness of manner or stillness. He is a tall thin boy with red hair, freckles and a crumpled, **ugly face**- which reflects his **ugly personality**. Ralph tells Piggy that his job is to take the boys' names; a more positive and motivating way of dealing with Piggy than Jack's dismissiveness.

Jack is the only character who has an identifiable surname (Merridew). He thinks that calling people by their surnames (a public school convention) is more adult, but in fact it is just more formal and less personal.

Much of the tone of the opening chapter reflects **Ralph**'s relaxed, happy mood. He thinks that the island, which he describes (in the next chapter) as a coral island, is the place of his dreams, where there is fun to be had- words like happy, excited, laughing, leaping, triumphant, shining and exploring convey how positive he feels. He **tries to get away from Piggy, but their joint discovery of the conch binds them together.**

The landscape of the scene in front of us is bright and exotic. The forest, the palm trees, the lagoon, the beach, the platform and the swimming pool formed within the beach all seem pleasant enough. But Golding includes the odd, ominous discord- the bird Ralph disturbs has a witch-like cry, the coconuts are skull-like, the birds cry, the waves make a grinding, roaring sound, animals squeal, and the conch strikes a harsh note. These are not the sounds of Paradise.

More than this, the forest, though it has no words, is alive; and vibrates minutely. The character of the island, and its hostility to human invasion, is apparent when the Lord of the Flies speaks to Simon at the end of Chapter 8.

The heat is intense and relentless. The boys will feel this in difficult ways as the novel develops. In Chapter 4, we learn that there are sharks between the shore and the coral reef, and that the island is in the Pacific Ocean.

Why are groups of British schoolboys wearing their home uniforms, so far away? How has a poor working-class boy like Piggy gone on a trip like this, to the other side of the world? These are among many unanswered questions.

We cannot test the information we are given about how the boys came to be here against any standard of realism. A large number of boys, from different schools, but all wearing school uniforms, was being flown out of an area where an atom bomb had been dropped. Their plane was attacked, and went down in flames. Yet there is no wreckage either on shore or in the sea. There are no injured boys. There are no crew. Nor does the shock of the danger they have been in seem to have had any effect on any of the boys.

Because it would be inconvenient for Golding to start his story with this type of realism, he simply omits it; the landing is not important, only how they tackle the issues of survival and rescue.

The other unsatisfactory piece of technique is Golding's description of the twins, Sam and Eric. Throughout the novel, he treats the issue of twinhood as something odd and undifferentiated. Look carefully at his description here, in Chapter 1, when he first introduces us to the two boys; do you agree that it is simplistic and dated?

The action in the chapter is both strong and necessary; Ralph and Piggy meet, they find the conch, Ralph is chosen as leader, and he, Jack and Simon discover together that they are on an uninhabited island; so there is no means of escape, or of communicating with the outside world.

The chapter ends with the failure to kill the trapped piglet. Ralph challenges Jack to explain why he didn't kill it, and Golding explains, as narrator (her, on Jack's behalf), that they cannot yet adjust to the "enormity" of killing (because, **once you have killed a pig, what is to stop you from killing a boy who is like a pig- Piggy- or anyone else?**). And, as Jack threatens, with prophetic and dramatic irony, next time there will be no mercy for the victim at the end of his knife.

Chapter 2

A second assembly follows on from the exploration of the island which derived from the first assembly in the morning. The heat has burnt most of the children, and the choirboys have put their cloaks aside; the new location calls for new types of behaviour.

Ralph explains the situation; Jack, excitably, interrupts him with his own agenda about **hunting pigs**, which **is already a fixation** of his. Allowing him to define his role as being in charge of the hunters will prove to be a costly mistake. Ralph defines the need for rules, and how **the conch will be used to**

support democratic debate and discussion. Again, Jack is interested only in the opportunity to inflict violent punishment on any rule-breakers.

Piggy and Ralph point out that, because their plane was shot down on its journey, their location will not be known to anyone; so it may be some time before they are rescued. But they are not sad or frightened – they feel that the island is a good place.

The positive tone is undermined, when the small boy with the birthmark on his face reluctantly raises the problem of a large creature which appears at night. He calls it both a snake and a beastie, and the older boys- who know the difference between a bad dream and reality- understand that this is the former.

Even so, Ralph cannot reassure the younger children, by denying its existence. Jack tries to reassure them using a different approach. He promises that, if it does exist, he will hunt and kill it. By doing this, he allows for the force of irrational fears in a way Ralph cannot, because he is more hot-headed and less rational than Ralph.

When, for the first time (of many), Ralph raises the need for a signal fire, **Jack leads the excited crowd or mob** away, and **Ralph and Piggy are left, with the conch**, to bemoan the boys' childish behaviour. **This prefigures the way Ralph and Piggy have the conch, but less and less power, from Chapter 8 onwards**. Piggy- with unintended irony- complains that they are behaving like a crowd of kids- which is exactly what they are!

Because Jack has had an opportunity to lead the boys up to where the fire is to be made, he can collaborate with Ralph in moving the key log into position. **They cooperate**, too, by taking Piggy's glasses as a way of lighting a fire, as they know no other method. The fire has too much heat, and no smoke; **Jack bullies Piggy, puts him down, and intimidates him**, when he tries to intervene. There is dramatic irony in **Jack**'s announcement that they are not savages because they are English, because public school boy Jack **is the most English and the most savage of all the boys**.

Jack promises to be responsible for the fire and the watch for ships, by using the choir to do those jobs. The need for coordinated and organised tasks comes from the need to be rescued. Roger pessimistically predicts that they may never be rescued; he is the boy who comes to behave without regard to any normal social rules, and is delighted to find that he can indulge his own sadism. Look for the evidence of that in chapters 11 and 12.

While **Piggy tries**, again, **to advise on how to build a sustainable fire**, the one they have made goes wild and out of control, and turns the forest below them savage. Ralph, in turn, feels savage or anarchic, and he fails to support **Piggy**, who **has to point out that the consequence of their unruly and disorganised behaviour is almost certainly that the small boy with the birthmark has been burnt alive.**

Chapter 2 builds on and extends **the potential for conflict between the democratic leader, Ralph, and the demagogic Jack**. It shows us how hard it is to organise a mob (even of small children) or calm its irrational fears. And it shows us that, whatever is done to the island, the island will give back to those who do it. **Rolling rocks, starting fires, and killing pigs all provoke the island to reject its tiresome colonists**, and inflict the same chaos and suffering on them.

Piggy relies on the conch as the only way he can secure a hearing; it dies with him, in Chapter 11.

Fire is really Ralph's pet subject (as hunting is Jack's). He insists that without a fire there can be no rescue. He is proved correct, in that the massive fire in Chapter 12 leads to the dramatic rescue and saves him from Jack. But, as the prospect of rescue fades (because the other boys fail to provide support for it), fire becomes, for Ralph, a comfort in distress- until Jack steals it from him as part of his revolution and his overturning, first, of Ralph's authority, and then of his right to life.

For Jack, Roger and the hunters, fire is a means of cooking meat. They have neither the desire nor the imagination to work towards being rescued; they are driven by excitement and short-term appetite, and will not defer their own gratification, or work towards a longer-term goal (which is why they do not have shelters). **For them, fire is primitive, a return to pre-civilised times; for Ralph, fire should be a means of communicating with the outside world and therefore the means of salvation.**

Chapter 3

Some time has passed since the end of chapter 2, because **Jack**'s hair has grown much longer and his skin is much more freckled and sunburnt. He still has not managed to kill a pig, although he behaves like a native hunter and has a sharp stick for a spear (not just a knife). Is it his lack of success, or his regressing to a more primitive way of living, which is making him nearly mad with frustration? In Chapter 1, we read that he **is always on the verge of anger- he is emotionally unstable**, and so less well equipped to lead than he supposes. Now he is hunting on his own; it is unsurprising that, without help, he cannot outwit and trap a wild pig.

He expects Ralph to acknowledge his efforts, as your leader should; but Ralph is preoccupied by the impossible task of building a shelter with only Simon to help him. Simon points out to Ralph that he should tell the other boys to help, but he is too lax with them; Ralph points out to Jack that some of his hunters are not watching the fire, but swimming, because Jack allowed them to leave their post.

Leaders have to award their approval to results; and **Jack's ongoing failure to hunt anything successfully means that Ralph will continue to express dissatisfaction with him.**

Both boys are frustrated at their own inability to complete the difficult task they have set themselves; they are angry with each other, but they cannot resolve their differences, only put them aside for the moment (so that the pile of differences constantly grows bigger).

Simon begins to take on an important role now. He has no ambition to be the leader himself, but he confronts Ralph with his own weaknesses, and is attuned to the difficulties- both of building shelters and of the mood of fear among the smallest children, which makes shelters (the ones they have not yet built) even more valuable, as a source of safety.

He raises the perception that perhaps the island is not "good"- contrary to Ralph's own view- and Jack admits that he can feel hunted while he is hunting- as if there is a hostile presence in the jungle, and they are unwelcome there. This prefigures a theme which grows stronger in later chapters- **the island resents and rejects those who behave badly on it.**

Ralph judges that Simon is odd. He has gone off into the forest by himself. The last part of Chapter 3 is devoted to Simon and his need for solitude (like Christ going into the wilderness for Lent).

Simon's route into the forest is familiar, because he goes there, followed by the younger children, for whom he picks the best and ripest fruit from the branches they cannot reach, among acres of fruit trees.

He goes past there, deeper into the forest, to a darker, cooler place, and then on to a hot, light, aromatic open space, where he hides, and seems to do nothing.

Golding describes him now as a small, skinny boy with bright eyes and a pointed chin. This adds to the brief detail in Chapter 1, where he fell in the sand on his face, fainting, and was described as having thick, rough, straight black hair which hung down. He is a loner, but a brave, wise and reassuring figure- as we shall see.

Jack is so obsessed with hunting the pig that he has almost forgotten the concept of rescue. In their focus and motivation, Jack and Ralph are worlds apart.

Chapter 4

The writing is this chapter is very taut and tense; and Golding manages to clarify for us some of his key themes and ideas.

Note the threatening language Golding uses in the first two paragraphs, to create a sense of foreboding- snapping, angry, menaced, dark, darkness.

Piggy understands what a mirage is, and how science can explain the apparently inexplicable, such as optical illusions. Later in the chapter, we are told that Piggy is like a young stag, but that baldness is his natural condition. He is a young fogey, old before his time; he **constantly supports Ralph's aims (even when Ralph himself is tired of serious thought and of the idea of rescue) and he does not take offence when he is ridiculed even by those who should be appreciative of his efforts**.

It is a significant detail that **Piggy is the only boy whose hair stays the same length - this, of course, is not literally possible, but it suggests that he is not growing; that he has already reached a point of maturity beyond the others.**

In this chapter, Golding examines why Roger and Piggy are both outsiders. Roger is a deeply secretive, unpleasant and even evil boy; Piggy is boring, dull, lazy physically, and weakened by asthma and short-sightedness- and therefore a figure of fun and derision. The comparison makes us think. Is the tendency to bully or tease someone like Piggy the same as throwing stones at someone like the six-year old Henry? Where is the line between "harmless" leg pulling and unacceptable cruelty?

Golding brings on to the stage of the narrative two more of the six-year-olds- first Percival, then Henry- to show how uninterested in, and indifferent to, shaping the society we live in some people are. **Percival is in a state of continual distress, crying and fearful; he is the same colour as a mouse (and like a mouse in how timid and fearful he is); even his own mother had not found him appealing; he is a natural victim (like Piggy, but more so) and boys kick sand in his eyes.**

Just as the character of Simon started to be developed in Chapter 3, so, here, is Roger's. He (and Maurice) destroy the youngest boys' sandcastles, for no other reason than they can. **Maurice is reined in from behaving really badly because his parents had smacked him for being aggressive to other children; bullying met with punishment. The memory he has- of being made to accept guilt for what he had done wrong- still affects his behaviour, and he makes an excuse, and chooses not to be cruel, because he is not as nasty as Roger.**

Roger's skin colour is not much changed by the sun; this implies that he spends most of his time in the shade or shadows, watching or stalking others; he is anti-social.

Look back at how Golding introduced him in Chapter 1- as a boy who keeps out of the way and has no friends. His hair matches his gloomy expression, in Chapter 2, when he had made the prediction that there might never be any rescue or escape. Now, his alienation from the group is becoming fiercer and harsher. He follows Henry, who is playing with the tiny creatures washed up with the waves, and enjoying directing them and controlling them – **even the youngest, Golding is saying, have a desire to impose their authority on something smaller and weaker than themselves; it is an innate instinct** (do you agree?).

Roger is a psychopath who feels no attachment to society or empathy with the weak. When he somehow fails to be injured by coconuts which fall from sixty feet above him, he does not feel relieved, or lucky, or anything. Instead, he starts throwing stones towards Henry; not, at this stage, to hit him, but to miss, narrowly, because he (like Maurice, but less forcefully) still feels the taboo of their old life- the social convention that hurting other people is wrong. Henry thus has a protected zone of three yards on each side of him, which Roger will not throw stones into.

In Chapter 11, he will kill Piggy, by dropping a huge stone too close to him. By that point, the residual constraints of a civilised society have worn off and there is no deterrent to Roger's sadistic drive.

Roger still hides when he thinks Henry may see him. **His thinly restrained desire to inflict harm and pain is a guilty secret which he wants to keep to himself. He is interested in being violent without being accountable for it.**

Jack then includes Roger in the semi-secret and experimental ritual of putting on warpaint. He thinks this will confuse the pigs and put them off their guard during the hunts. The effect of **the paint**, though, is to make Jack feel a different person - and it **changes him**, instantly, **into a dancing, snarling, bloodthirsty savage. Golding says that Jack is "liberated from shame and self-consciousness"-** the mask allows him to regress to a more primitive version of himself, ungoverned by any sense of morality. The boys who face him when he is dressed this way are frightened and appalled, but Sam and Eric feel forced to obey Jack's command- it gives him a fierce new authority, and makes him a stronger opponent for Ralph.

After a lull, during which Ralph, Piggy, Simon and Maurice are doing very little, Ralph suddenly sees smoke from a ship's funnel on the horizon. He is so desperate to be rescued! He assumes that the ship will see the smoke from the fire and all will be well.

Piggy, then Simon, realise, before Ralph does, that they have no smoke to attract the attention of the ship. A frantic chase up the mountain reveals what we already know- that the fire has gone out, because no one has kept it going. We know that tending the fire was a responsibility Jack had volunteered to take on; and the hunters are visible below, near the beach. This time, they have managed to kill a pig. They walk in a procession and sing a simple, violent chant.

Jack is euphoric because the paint has worked and he has managed a kill. Like Henry, Jack has a desire to impose his will on living things; but, because of his obsession with proving himself, and the role he has taken on, his test has been whether he would be strong and ruthless enough to kill the animal. The collective failure to kill a pig at the end of Chapter 1 became Jack's personal failure in Chapter 3, where Ralph goaded him about it; so, to some extent, Jack's triumph (and the lack of restraint, the borderline he has crossed) is the result of Ralph's attitude. But **the need for meat is less acute than the need for rescue, and Jack and the hunters have broken their promise to maintain the fire** (look back at how clearly Jack made that promise, near the end of chapter 2).

Ralph is interested only in the failure to be rescued, so, when he confronts Jack with his failure to keep his promise, and the consequence of that, his voice is loud and savage (in fact, if the fire had been lit, the novel would have had to end with a rescue here in Chapter 4!).

Jack is embarrassed at his mistake, and he goes on to apologise for it. But, before this, he and Ralph face each other, and **Jack stands for the irrational, the easily distracted, the impulsive, the emotional, the self-absorbed, while Ralph stands for the big picture of long-term plans and goals and rational thinking. It seems impossible to keep both aspects of our being in balance.**

Piggy backs Ralph up, in accusing Jack of breaking his promise; Jack punches him and hits him (he would not hit Ralph), **and his glasses are broken**. Amid the playground mockery, the serious point is a symbolic one- Piggy's insights are not valued, and **Piggy himself will be smashed on the rocks** (in Chapter 11).

Simon- who is a barometer of what is about to happen in the near future- appears to be afraid, before Ralph and Jack meet; this points to a fundamental and unfixable conflict between them. The narrative comment confirms that things are going badly wrong; the collaboration is breaking down; Jack's unthinking mistake is unforgivable, because of what it has cost (the chance of rescue). **Ralph** cannot excuse or forgive that irresponsible behaviour, and so he **and Jack are on different sides of the fence, as they will be, now, for the rest of the novel.**

In Chapter 2, **Ralph had lit the fire with Piggy's glasses, and Jack had helped** to fan it and keep it going. **Now, Ralph re-lights it, but Jack is not involved.** Jack tries to be cruel to Piggy, again, claiming that, because he did not hunt, he is not entitled to eat. Simon gives Piggy his own meat, to prevent Piggy from being humiliated and bullied.

The killing of the pig is re-enacted, with Maurice pretending to be the pig, **in a way which chillingly prefigures the killing**

of Simon in Chapter 9. The celebration, and the atmosphere of a camp, cannot obscure the fundamental question of who is in charge and what the priorities are; so Ralph announces that he is calling an assembly, and he marches back down the mountain.

Chapter 5

This chapter deals with the assembly- the first one which is held in near-darkness. It breaks up in disorder, because, although Ralph still sees the need for organisation, and argues for the necessary things to be done, the boys are starting to protest that he is making **too many rules** (specifically, a new one that- because Jack and the hunters failed to keep the fire alight- all cooking must be done on the mountain, not on the beach).

The attempt to resolve the question of what they are afraid of fails.

Ralph, Jack and Piggy all try to show that there is no evidence for a physical beast or a harmful, malevolent presence on the island.

Ultimately, though, **intellectual knowledge cannot outweigh irrational thoughts and feelings**.

The unwritten rule that the impulsive glamour and excitement of hunting will always overpower the mundane need to build shelters and keep a fire burning had led to the irreconcilable confrontation between Ralph and Jack at the end of the last chapter; this chapter reinforces that message.

Before the assembly begins, Ralph reflects on his own role, and his relationship with Piggy. He knows that leadership is about making wise decisions, which are thought through, not improvised. He sees that **Piggy can think, although otherwise he lacks the attributes of a chief. As Ralph becomes more and more frustrated and demoralised by the boys' failure to follow his lead, he relies on Piggy, for support, then ideas, then friendship**. Here, Piggy stands on the edge of the assembly at first, because he disapproves of it; but he is soon drawn into it. Like Ralph, he cannot lay the boys' irrational fears to rest.

The chapter opens with an explanation of Ralph's thoughts. He is beginning to feel uncomfortable on the island, and that happiness has been lost; this is why he wants to confront and deal with the fears which are distracting the boys from the purposeful action they need to take- all the things (like keeping the fire alight, and building solid shelters) which are never done.

He tells the boys that they need to change how they behave, because decisions are not being followed through (letting the fire go out is the worst and most critical example); and because **fear is getting in the way of the structure and the happiness they started with.**

Jack criticises the younger boys for not hunting or helping, and says that they will simply have to put up with their fear- a typically unempathetic approach. He says that although his hunters talk about the existence of a beast, if it existed he would have seen it by now; so that fear is something they all experience, but there is no animal or creature they should be afraid of.

Piggy argues that fear is a type of ailment, and that there is no beast. But, he says- and he has been building up to this- we can be frightened of other people (as he is of Jack).

This point is lost in general derision, and Piggy invites the boys who are frightened to explain their fears. The first, Phil, explains that he had a nightmare about fighting creepers, but that when he woke up he was outside the shelter. Then he saw something grim moving in the trees. It emerges that this could have been Simon, because he had gone, during the night, to the place he knows in the jungle.

The second is the generally terrified Percival, who simply gives his name and address, and starts to cry; this sets off a general crying among the small boys. Percival then falls asleep, but only after Jack has heard him muttering that the beast comes from the sea- a possibility which cannot be disproved. There is speculation about what form a sea-monster might take. Then **Simon**- who is **always the voice of truth**- takes the conch.

Simon **says that perhaps there is a beast, but that the beast is "only us". In other words, the beast, the malevolent thing, is a part of our personality (as we have already seen with Roger and Jack, and even in Ralph's mild bullying of Piggy, as well as everyone else's), and Piggy is right to say that the only thing we should fear is other members of the same species.**

Simon is laughed aside, because he is inarticulate. Someone raises the idea of ghosts, and, in the dark, against a backdrop of talking palm trees which squeak in an evil way, order, and the discipline of speaking in turn, collapses.

When he feels forced to end the meeting with a vote on who believes in ghosts- and they do- Ralph feels that his leadership is failing. **Jack rebels openly, shouting his accusation that Ralph's rules are pointless** and that he always favours Piggy.

Piggy urges Ralph to blow the conch, to call the scattered crowd back to order from its mock hunting and chanting and howling. Ralph refuses to; he feels defeated, and that he ought to stand down. **Piggy points out that, without Ralph to protect him, Jack would do what he wanted to him, and hurt him, and he identifies- correctly- that Jack hates both of them.**

Simon instructs Ralph to continue; he repeats that he wants him to go on being chief and tells him to keep the fire going. If Ralph loses his motivation, the alternative is anarchy, with Jack unchallenged. The balance of power is tilting away from Ralph; **rather like the huge rock they rolled in Chapter 1, there is a moment of imbalance, just before a tide of destruction. Look back at that description and relate it, as a symbol, to this point in the plot of the novel.**

Chapter 6

The immediate issue- the boys' inability to focus on rescue because of their terror of the beast- becomes much more concrete because, that same night, **when everyone is asleep, a dead parachutist is blown on to the top of the island- precisely where the signal fire is kept- because an air battle is fought ten miles overhead.**

Note how Golding tells this part of the story- **we**, as readers, **know** all about the way the corpse and the parachute move, and where it has come to rest; we understand its grotesque leaning forward and straightening up. **The boys do not**.

We then watch while Sam and Eric discover it, in the half-light of the morning, as they re-light the fire. Notice the mention of the woodlice which cannot avoid being caught in the fire- **the boys are like small insects which cannot escape (from their own hot and destructive fears)**. Sam and Eric, like Ralph and Piggy, find the memory of the fire in Chapter 2 painful, because they feel guilty about the disappearance of the boy with the birthmark on his face.

Golding builds dramatic tension by delaying the discovery of the parachutist, and then presenting it, in a single sentence, where **we see not the corpse but the twins' horrified reaction to what they have seen**. Three short paragraphs expand on that response and fright- note the extensive use of alliteration (with words beginning with "f"), and the personification of the trees.

The twins give Ralph and Piggy a traumatised account of what they think they saw; it is so alarming that Ralph will not use the conch to call an assembly, for fear of bringing the beast down on them. The twins describe the beast to the assembly as a creature with wings, fur, teeth and claws, which pursued them on foot. The boys react with hysteria (Johnny), frank fear (Ralph) and avoidance (Piggy).

Jack is impatient to set out on a hunt for something more challenging than a pig; he is sarcastic, yet again, about what he sees as Ralph's bias in favour of keeping Piggy cosseted from danger. He openly disregards the authority of the conch, saying that only some boys (including him, of course) are fit to make decisions- not Simon or Bill or Walter.

Ralph corrects Jack- the project is not just a hunt (the beast may not leave tracks at all, from the description Sam and Eric have given); the fire needs to be reignited because the need for rescue is acute. Ralph insists on proper planning; they must search the unexplored end of the island first, and then go up the mountain to light the fire again.

We know that there is no beast in the sense they fear, and that the first part of the search will be futile. Jack takes a theatrical, self-dramatising role in the hunt, while Ralph tries to prepare himself for the burden of being the leader, which means he will have to do the dangerous part of the search himself.

The narrative finds time for two paragraphs about Simon, who walks alongside Ralph. Simon, the barometer of truth, knows that the beast cannot be as the twins described it. He does not know about the parachutist, yet; but he does sense that bravery and violence are the components of the beast in human nature. Perhaps we are at our most violent when we are called upon (as in a battle) to be unusually brave.

Simon absent-mindedly bumps into a tree, and a spot on his forehead starts to bleed. The same thing will happen to Ralph's bitten nail in Chapter 8. Because it happens to both boys, we can go on to make the plot link that a character who bleeds like this has been singled out for cruel suffering; Simon will be killed in Chapter 9, and Jack will attempt to murder Ralph in Chapters 11 and 12.

When the hunting party reaches the end of the island, Ralph decides to search, himself, even though Jack is the so-called hunter. **Simon** mutters that he **does not believe the beast is real**. The reader will sense, again, that Simon has a unique grasp of the truth, but this is not apparent to Ralph.

Golding pauses to describe the water alongside the fifteen-yard ledge of rock he has to walk along, the flat, table-shaped rock, and the breathing- style pattern of the rising and falling water. This is a way of **preparing the way for the moment of Piggy's death in chapter 11**, when he falls on to that rock.

Find the passage in Chapter 11 and compare it with the description here. Note, too, how Golding uses the sea to remove all traces of the dead- of the bodies of Simon, Piggy, the parachutist, and of the body of the aeroplane they crashed in.

Now, as though Simon's reassurance and knowledge has seeped through to him, Ralph realises that he did not expect to encounter a beast here. What he knows is beginning to catch up with what the reader knows and he does not.

Jack comes to join Ralph and he **is excited by the fort-like defences the rocks offer, and especially by the offensive damage the last of the precarious rocks could do to someone on the causeway a hundred feet below. This is precisely what Roger will do to Ralph and Piggy** at the fatal point in Chapter 11.

While Roger and the other boys are perfecting their rock-rolling- which seems innocent now, but will murder Piggy- Ralph has to insist on the need for the signal fire, and he is feeling the psychological strain of the effort of being the leader of a rabble with such a short attention span- they have forgotten about the beast already.

Chapter 7

This chapter ends with Ralph, Jack and Roger discovering the dead parachutist and running away, just as Sam and Eric had done at the end of Chapter 5. Once more, **the characters feel a sense of fear and nervousness which the reader, with our prior knowledge, does not. Instead, we can focus on the battle between Jack and Ralph. Each is trying to find a point at which the other's nerve or courage fails**. It is an attack initiated by Jack, as part of his constant campaign to expose Ralph as a leader inadequate to be their chief.

The chapter starts with a food break, which allows Ralph to think about the hugeness of the sea on this side of the island. It is worth analysing the language; Ralph feels oppressed, hopeless, pinned down. **Simon** appears at his elbow, to tell Ralph that he **is convinced that, in spite of his homesickness and his fading hopes of rescue, Ralph will get home**; Ralph seems to realise, finally, that Simon has a special connection with the truth, and that he is not really mad. Ralph's determination to continue as the leader- which safeguards the boys against Jack's primitivism- is stronger when he feels he may succeed, and weaker when he feels he will not.

An abortive hunt follows- Ralph is elated because he wounds the boar, and he is caught up in the excitement of hunting, just as Jack had been in Chapter 3. As readers, **we want Ralph not to be dragged down into the animalistic behaviour which drives Jack; but he very nearly is**.

Ralph's mind, made illogical by his dreams of home, tricks him into nonsensical thoughts (they are infantile- sucking his thumb, and pretending that the wild boar is the beast) and he is sucked into the hunters' ritualistic re-enactment, with Robert playing the part of the boar.

Golding presents Ralph here as being dangerously close to Roger and Jack, in his instinct for violence- he jabs at Robert with Eric's spear, and wants to hurt him. He only pulls back- pretending that the ritual was no more threatening than a game of rugby- when **Jack says, ominously, that the play-hunt needs to be made more authentic by dressing a small boy up as a pig (and killing them). This foreshadows what will be done to Piggy himself, and the hunting of Ralph in the final chapter**.

More particularly and specifically, **it anticipates the killing of Simon, where Ralph (and Piggy) are loosely attached to the murderous mob.** The language which Golding uses to describe Robert- squealed, blundered, screaming, struggling, frenzy, rump- blurs the distinction between the human and the sub-human (the pig). The reader is relieved to find that Ralph flirts with the dark, inhuman side, but withdraws, because he knows the limits of the "game".

The mountain still needs to be climbed, to search for the beast and attend to the fire. The boys are tired, and, as Jack points out, Piggy's glasses are with him, at the shelters, so they have no means to light a fire. Progress is slow; they need to let Piggy know that they will be returning later than they expected. Again, **Jack uses sarcasm to betray his hatred of Piggy (because he perceives that Ralph favours him). Simon volunteers to be the messenger- he has no fear of the beast, because he knows there is no such creature**. Jack sneers at Ralph, who recognises that Jack is trying to assert his own superiority as a leader. Jack's hot-headedness and obsessiveness create unnecessary risk, but Ralph cannot afford to lose the initiative, so he must accept every challenge to his authority and character.

Mindful of Piggy's motivating insight at the end of chapter 5- that he must continue as the leader, to keep Jack's hatred of him and Ralph in check- Ralph asks Jack directly why he hates him. Jack does not answer, because there is no reasonable answer. He simply falls back in the group and broods. Then he takes his revenge, by inviting (challenging) Ralph to go up the mountain with him, to look for the beast, even though they can do nothing with the fire.

Again, Ralph remains calm, and he rises to the challenge. Roger goes with them, because he would not be able to bear missing a fight. The ashes from the burnt-out fire are blinding. Ralph doubts there is a beast on top of the mountain- he is, subconsciously, fortified by what Simon has told him earlier. Jack's provocative and childish sarcasm and mind-games, together with his own exhaustion, make him angry; he lets Jack go first, while he and Roger sit next to the ashes of the fire.

Jack returns, almost unable to speak, he is so terrified. His account matches what Sam and Eric had seen. Ralph turns the tables on Jack by making him go back with him for another look. Jack hangs back while Ralph and Roger see the parachutist for themselves, from a distance of three or four yards; the twins had run away when they were fifteen yards away from the parachute, and heard a plopping noise which Jack has also described.

The three boys run away, just as Sam and Eric had done.

By giving us so much advance knowledge of what they would discover, Golding has sacrificed tension. He has moved the centre of the drama, so that it focuses on the

struggle between Jack's animalistic, thoughtless, impulsive style of leading- which comes from low self-esteem- and Ralph's more mature, calm, self-denying method. **We know that Golding wants us to side with Ralph because Simon is on Ralph's side.**

Whatever the opposition and difficulties, and however frustrating it feels, this way of leading protects the vulnerable by making the world a more stable and manageable place. The demagogues- the Jacks- need to be challenged. We shall see in the remainder of the novel what follows when that challenge fails.

Chapter 8

We have become accustomed to reading a style in this novel which presents events to us in a linear sequence, one after another. This chapter is different.

It starts the same evening, when Ralph and Jack have run back down to the shelters (though there is no sense of fright or panic). Jack calls an assembly to challenge Ralph as leader, and, when he fails, he goes off on his own. The assembly continues and Piggy suggests that they make a fire on the beach. At the same time, Simon goes on to the mountain, because he believes that they need to climb up it in order to confront their fears. **Simon sits in his secret place in the forest, while Piggy, Ralph and the twins feast on fruit (no** meat here) and Jack organises a particularly bloody and violent hunt, of the suckling sow.

When Jack leaves the sow's head, as a peace offering to the beast, it is impaled in Simon's clearing; dehydrated, he imagines that it is talking to him. Jack raids the new fire, with Maurice and Robert, and he appeals to the other boys to follow the meat and join him for a feast- in the hope that the bigger boys will desert. The chapter ends with a return to the sow's head, and Simon suffering a fit.

Golding needs two simultaneous story lines so that he can stage the killing of Simon, when he comes out of the forest; he has to have been separated from the rest of the boys, and he has to have a message which motivates his return.

How successfully Golding manages this is debatable; as we will see.

Piggy's role begins to change now. His initiative- setting up a fire by the shelters, so that the beast does not have to be faced- creates joy and a party atmosphere. **He lights the fire himself; he provides food, proactively, for Ralph; he brings wood for the fire; he feels liberated by the departure of Jack**, whom he refers to as "a certain person". He is convinced that the residue of boys, without Jack, will be happy; he sees that **Ralph is accepting him as a friend and relying on him more.**

Ralph knows that the boys will not fight the creature they saw; it is too big, and it seems too malevolent. He feels defeated, and he has no appetite for more talking. Jack steps into the vacuum to accuse Ralph of being like Piggy, of being a coward, and not a proper leader, but his challenge ends in a silent, humiliating defeat. **Simon** is handicapped by his fear of speaking to a group, but he **suggests, simply, that climbing the mountain- to see the beast for themselves- is the only thing they can do**. The boys are too fearful to agree, so Simon is left to carry out his suggestion by himself.

Piggy's idea, of building the fire on the rocks, and Jack's, of appeasing the beast with an offering of meat, are both designed to avoid facing reality.

The problem with this is that it leaves unresolved the irrational fears the boys have- and that leads them to kill Simon in a frenzy of mob violence.

None of the boys is exempt from the guilt and responsibility for this murder- not even Ralph and Piggy. In the narrative, Golding points out that, where fears are unresolved, there is little to distinguish panic and hysteria from dynamism and a positive outlook. A sensible, optimistic attitude can soon become timid and hopeless, unless we keep the fire burning, and refuse to give our fears power over our thoughts.

Reality bites when Ralph realises that, to keep the fire up, there is only Piggy, the twins and him- Maurice, Bill and Roger have all gone to the hunters' camp.

Jack takes the hunters into the forest, where, now, they are nervous. He is happy, because he has a group which he can lead in his own right; and he has a plan to induce more of the bigger boys to join him. **The hunt is like a military operation. Jack has improved his equipment; the spears have fire-hardened points, to make them sharper. He has developed sophisticated skills in tracking, so that his prey cannot escape; this ominously foreshadows how he will hunt Ralph in the final chapter.**

The sow sheds drops of blood, and Ralph has (just) noticed his own bitten nail bleeding.

The scene of the killing is in Simon's clearing, with its butterflies and flowers. The narrative is told partly from the sow's point of view. Golding couples this with a graphic account of the pitiless violence Jack and Ralph bring to the killing; the quantities and the smell of the blood.

Roger addresses Jack as "chief" (Ralph has needed no such title), and he points out that they have no means of lighting a fire to cook the meat. **Jack** already plans to steal fire from Ralph and Piggy.

He **instructs Roger to sharpen a stick at both ends, and he impales the sow's head on the stick, as an offering to the beast. Roger has prepared a similar stick for hunting Ralph in Chapter 12; the implication is that he too will be decapitated, after being put to death in a sadistic way. For Jack and Roger, killing pigs and killing people will, by then, have become the same thing.** The hunters leave with the sow's carcass.

Now we have the first passage with Simon and the sow's head- which is the "gift for the darkness" of the chapter's title.

The head is grinning, amused and cynical; detached from its own death. The flies, which are feasting on the sow's discarded guts, feast on Simon's sweat, too- although he is alive.

The head is therefore given the title "Lord of the Flies".

Simon, we are told, recognises something ancient in it- presumably, the fact that all humans and all animals will die, in their own turn, so that what we tend to think distinguishes mankind from the animal world may be a way of flattering ourselves; **we are all savages under the skin.**

Back on the beach, the oppressive heat (which Simon feels too) threatens a thunderstorm. Ralph complains to Piggy about the boys' lack of responsibility, which leads them to ignore the importance of the fire- their only hope of survival in the long term. Then Jack's gang of painted savages comes to steal lighted branches for their own fire. **Jack is using paint instead of clothes, in a further step back to primitivism. He insists on a bizarre ritual, too, where, when he has finished speaking, his henchmen (Maurice and Robert) confirm, in unison, that "the Chief has spoken".**

Ralph now finds it hard to speak to the other boys; he is emotionally exhausted, but he still **feels the acute difference between living as a savage (which is easy) and keeping the fire up (which is almost impossible, because it requires patience, dedication, discipline and self-sacrifice).**

The boys cannot resist the appeal of meat. Golding has to engineer this, in order to make Simon's murder a crime for which the whole of this increasingly uncivilised society must take the responsibility and blame.

In the final short section of this chapter, **the Lord of the Flies (that is to say the dead sow's head) tells Simon that it is the Beast.** (Or rather, a dehydrated and confused Simon thinks this is what is happening).

Pigs can be hunted, and killed violently, as an outlet for the instinct to be violent, but the instinct to kill is within every human being. It also tells Simon that he must go back to the other boys, where he will be killed; and that

he, Simon, is not wanted, and will be killed, for fun, by Jack, Roger, Maurice, Robert, Bill, Piggy and Ralph.

This core of coherent sense is wrapped up in other insulting and patronising talk by the sow's head which means little, is obscure, and seems arbitrary; why should it call Simon silly? Simon is the wrong boy to accuse of misunderstanding what the beast actually is. Simon has neither misbehaved nor challenged the sow's head.

The writing here seems unnatural and mannered to me. I find this a weak section of the book, which is a shame, because it is from this section that the book takes its title and thus much of its symbolic meaning.

Of course, it is difficult to give a dead pig a convincing voice, but, if it is the voice of an unspoken truth, it is important that the author speaks in that voice clearly and with weight. I find the writing here rather trivialised, even infantile; certainly it is not resonant. You could cut it out, in a way, for what it tells us about anything – it is needed purely as a plot device. For sure, Simon does not need to be told what the beast is; of all the boys, he is the one who already knows.

Chapter 9

This is the shortest chapter in the novel, and one of the most dramatic. In the teeth of a storm, **the two beings perceived as**

the beast – Simon and the parachutist- are removed from the island, which leaves the real beast- the inner savagery of the individual (and the group) – to reveal its true force.

The other element here is the contrast between Jack's leadership style and Ralph's.

Simon suffers a heat-induced blackout which involves a severe nose-bleed; this contributes to his beast-like or non-human appearance when he emerges from the forest later, although there is no real description of his physical appearance at that point.

When he recovers consciousness, he reiterates the words he had muttered to the assembly; the only thing to be done is to confront the creature which has terrified the twins, Ralph, Jack and Roger. Simon's eyes have lost their brightness, and he walks like an old man. He is expressionless; the boyishness has gone.

Simon is the only boy brave enough to confront the parachutist on his own, and to do something about it. The flies plague the corpse, as they do the sow's head. Simon observes, takes action and makes judgments; Golding does not pay any attention to his thoughts or feelings. His reaction to the corpse is not shock or fear; he is sick, but, instead of running away, he releases the parachute lines from the trees. He judges that **the beast is harmless and horrible,** and that he must convey that message to the boys, who seem to have moved their camp (to Jack's end of the beach).

The scene shifts to the beach, so that Golding can prepare the weather for the killing of Simon (looming sky, warmer than blood, pained/pain; further on, thunderous, storm coming, the threat of violence, struck, blows of the thunder, dark and terrible) and motivate Ralph's and Piggy's decision to join the other boys. **Ralph understands that acting as a tribe, with war-paint and hunting, has a seductive attraction beyond the appeal of meat**.

We know, with Ralph, that it will be difficult to bring those boys back. We know- Ralph doesn't- that Jack intends to use the feast to get more of the boys over to his side, because he had announced that- to the boys already with him- in the previous chapter.

The reluctant journey Ralph and Piggy make, to observe Jack's camp and experience his authoritarian power, anticipates the powerless trip they will make later to try to recover Piggy's broken glasses.

Jack looks like a figure from a film documentary about hidden tribes in remote parts of the world- he is painted and wearing flower garlands, and he sits like an idol on a log which he pretends is his throne. He expects to be treated as a god or a king, and issues orders, in a mixture of imperatives and rhetorical questions.

This narcissistic leadership style is artificial, undemocratic and vain. Golding adds his own condemnation- he shows that **we are to view Jack as a Neanderthal or caveman,** because he says that "authority….chattered in his ear like an ape".

There is an awkward silence when Ralph and Piggy arrive, because of the conflict and tension that comes with them (it is useful to **go through the whole novel looking at how Golding uses silence as a means of heightening dramatic tension**). Piggy is burnt, accidentally, by a piece of hot meat; this piece of **slapstick physical comedy defuses the** situation, just as Maurice had relieved the terror of the younger boys in chapter 5 by pretending to fall over.

Jack orders meat to be given to Ralph and Piggy. After the eating, he **issues the invitation to join his tribe, which we knew was coming, but Ralph and Piggy did not. Jack's appeal- that he will provide meat and will protect the boys from the beast- is now more effective and powerful than Ralph's reminder that hunting is a subsidiary task, and that the conch (democratic and organised society) should govern what they do. Ralph does not manage to remind the crowd about the need to be rescued; Piggy knows they are defeated. This decisive confrontation is supported by thunder. Ralph's leadership is being destroyed.**

As the rain starts, Ralph- now whining sarcastically (as Jack had done), rather than leading- goads the deserters about the fact they have no shelters. Jack's answer is the same as always- violent physical activity, either in calling a hunt, or, as here, calling for the ritualistic hunting dance to be played out.

Golding adds flashes of lightning to make the scene more dramatic. Roger acts as the pig, and there is a wider range of weapons now- wooden clubs and spits as well as spears.

Even Ralph and Piggy are drawn to the group, because all of us feel the need to be "attached" to a social unit (parents, or family, or whatever is the nearest equivalent available).

Clearly, this group is wrong in its standards of behaviour. But being inside it is safer and more comfortable than being outside it. Golding wants to include Ralph and Piggy so that he can put forward the view that the beast- the instinct for inhumane violence- is societal and collective,

not just something which abnormal or damaged individuals are prone to.

The function or benefit of the group, however wild it is, is that it allows the individual relief from what Golding has called, earlier, the "hell" of their irrational fear. It is that fear which leads to the breaking down of the understandable and lawful world (Chapter 5); but **escape into the group makes the individual anonymous, and able to avoid personal responsibility- just as no member of the group took responsibility for the death in the fire of the boy with the facial birthmark in Chapter 2.**

When Roger gives up the role of pig, there is a gap in the ring, and we remember Jack's sinister suggestion in Chapter 7 that they should use a small boy. The mob develops a collective character of its own- it is "a single organism", with a mechanistic, dehumanised throb - a phrase which applies both to people and to machines, which have no mind of their own.

The intensity of the thunder and lightning intensifies the chant, and the intense fear- according to Golding- releases an intense desire to kill. This is a psychological insight which comes from the battlefields of the Second World War.

The attack on Simon is short and brutal. He is referred to, once, as "Simon", to identify him, but seven times as the beast and four times by "it". At the moment Simon is killed, the wind lifts the parachutist from the top of the mountain down on to the beach and out to sea.

After the storm has died out, Simon is referred to initially as   a beast, and then finally he is personified again, as Simon's dead body.

Group hysteria over the fire had led to the accidental death of the small boy in Chapter 2; now it has taken on a more primitive and savage character, so that **collective fear- in the absence of shelters- has become the trigger for a ritualistic murder.**

That fear is the fear of being hunted by the beast; but the fear itself releases the beast, because, as the Lord of the Flies (the dead pig's head that Simon imagined was speaking to him) **had said at the end of Chapter 8, "I'm part of you".**

Chapter 10

We see **Ralph's psychological deterioration. The transfer of power to Jack becomes final and complete with the theft of Piggy's glasses**. At both ends of the island, the boys have to deal with the knowledge that Simon has been killed.

The first scene in this chapter shows us **Ralph** scruffier and more traumatised and isolated than before. He **is no longer the boy with fair hair and the golden body; he limps and has various bits of physical damage.**

All the bigger boys, apart from the twins and Piggy, have defected to Jack. **Ralph and Piggy discuss Simon's death.**

Ralph recognises that it was murder, and that they should now be more scared than ever, because the last constraint against savagery has been broken. He is right to be afraid not of the beast but "of us"- of the group's collective

capacity for savagery (particularly under Jack's style of rule).

Piggy, who is rational and sceptical, and does not really believe in the beast, tries to argue that Simon's death was a pretence, or an accident, and/or that he provoked it himself by the way he came crawling on to the beach in the dark, so that it was natural to mistake him for the beast (this is nonsense).

Piggy does not want to acknowledge that the rule of law has broken down; he has already expressed his intuitive understanding that, because Jack hates him and Ralph, he will hurt them if he has the opportunity; which, as leader, he will now have.

He seems to find the idea that a mob can develop its own psychology or personality an alien concept. He still clings to the old comforts- the idea that they will maintain a fire, and that Ralph is still their leader- when the evidence suggests otherwise; Ralph knows how difficult it will be for just four boys to keep a fire going, and Eric complains, almost immediately, of being too tired to do so.

Sam and Eric have been trying to avoid Ralph, in order to avoid the issue of Simon. There is a rare touch of humour as the four boys discuss the dance that none of them had attended, as they make clear their absence of involvement, in **the unspoken knowledge that Simon's death was in fact murder.**

Golding switches the action to Jack's camp, so that we can see how Simon's death is dealt with there. They have moved to Castle Rock, as it is the safest place to resist the horrors of the island.

Roger hears that Jack has ordered an apparently arbitrary and random beating for a boy called Wilfred; such unchecked intimidation (the technique of a tyrant who governs by fear) appeals to him, but Golding calls it an irresponsible use of power. Jack issues orders about keeping watch (but not keeping and watching a fire- he has no interest in rescue), and mentions that the beast may try to attack them.

He identifies Simon as the beast in disguise, and says that the offering of the pig's head may not be enough to guarantee that the beast leaves them alone. One boy- Stanley- half-formulates the question of how the beast can still be alive if they killed Simon; **Jack** simply refutes the knowledge that they did kill him. He now **presents the beast as something unpredictable, still alive, and which they cannot kill. This is because a threat from the beast can only help Jack to maintain order. It also confirms what the Lord of the Flies had said to Simon- that the inner beast, the real beast, is not something you can kill, because you cannot kill what is inside you.**

Just as Jack's intention to get the older boys to defect to him was known to the reader before it became clear to Ralph, now Jack announces that he, Maurice and Roger will raid Ralph's camp for fire that night, so that they can cook tomorrow's kill.

The scene switches back to Ralph, Piggy and the twins. Their fire is now a comfort as much as a signal to possible rescuers. Ralph rules out a proactive attempt to escape from the island on the grounds that they might be captured by "the reds" (meaning that the war is being waged by Communists on the one side and the English and/or their allies on the other).

Eric suggests that being a prisoner of war would be preferable to being a prisoner of Jack- ironically, as he and Sam will be seized by Jack in the next chapter. He does not refer to the other boys by name- they are now too primitive and savage to have civilised names or individual identities any more.

Ralph has forgotten or lost his old power to motivate Sam and Eric to keep the fire going; **the fire is dying, and his passion, his belief that their fate is in their own hands at all, is dying with it. One of the consequences of Jack's supremacy is that fire will only be used for cooking- and, in Chapter 12, for smoking out the prey you hunt (Ralph).**

The fire is left out overnight. This is a plot device, because it means that Jack's raid cannot succeed by taking lit branches out of the fire- they have to take Piggy's glasses, which are the only means of lighting a fire anywhere on the island.

Ralph is fantasising every night about being safely back in England. Escapism is the only means left to him of retaining his sanity. The way he talks to Piggy, and some of his physical movements, show that he is **on the verge of a breakdown.**

The four boys are a disturbed, vulnerable, disorganised and dishevelled rabble. When Jack's attack comes (a surprise to them, but not to us) Golding takes care to show us that the new injuries they sustain are partly self-inflicted.

Ralph and Eric have been fighting and hurting each other by mistake. Piggy, with his over-attachment to what is outmoded, assumes that Jack had come to take the conch. But the conch has no value to Jack- it is a redundant symbol of a civilised method of behaving and organising, which is alien to him.

Piggy and Ralph finally realise what we already knew- the aim of the raid was to take Piggy's glasses, and the boys defending them would be too weak not to suffer another routine defeat.

Chapter 11

With no means to light a fire, Ralph, Piggy and he twins are in a hopeless situation. They enact **a weak and rather pathetic assembly, where it is clear that Ralph's memory is disintegrating in the same way that the forces of civilisation are.**

Piggy now accepts that Simon was murdered, and Ralph- rightly- holds Jack responsible for that event. Ralph repeatedly asserts that they are not savages, and that therefore his group will not resort to painting their faces.

Ralph no longer claims to lead, but offers to go with Piggy on his mission to recover his glasses. We see how pathetically unable to see Piggy is without them; he cannot see more than about two feet away, and has to be helped to find fruit to pick.

The boys' appeal to Jack will be on the grounds of morality, or what is "right". The reader has a sense of foreboding; any hope we have that Jack might do the decent thing is far outweighed by our rational knowledge that his brutal character will simply humiliate them.

We are very aware of Jack's hatred of Piggy and Ralph, as well as what Golding has called "the possibilities of

irresponsible authority"- the opportunity to be as murderous, vicious and cruel as he likes.

Where repeating phrases in the assemblies used to be a way of securing understanding and agreement, the smaller assembly (of the four older boys and some small ones) convinces no-one; it is just a way of trying to cling to what has been comforting in the past.

Piggy is right to feel that it is morally offensive that Jack has stolen their fire and rendered him unable to see. He demands action because he is so vulnerable without his sight. Ralph completes the moral picture- he would have shared the means of making fire, and under Jack's leadership there will never be any chance of rescue.

Piggy is so outraged that he now refers to him by his first and second name; he is no longer just Jack. He is a tyrant and Piggy is so desperate to get his glasses back that this basic desire to see outweighs his fear of him.

Ralph has the desperate and pathetic idea that if they dressed smartly, as they used to, Jack might feel obliged to play the game by the old rules (of fairness and respect for others); but they cannot revert to that as a way of showing that they are different.

As Jack struggles with his fading memory, Golding inserts into the narrative an oblique and intriguing puzzle. He says that **Jack remembered something that Simon had said to him once, by the rocks**.

"The rocks" is a vague location; there are rocks near the assembly point, as well as elsewhere. So this gives us a choice of situations to think back on. What had Simon said to Ralph? He had said that perhaps there is a beast, but it is only us

(Ralph knows this, and has already expressed it); that the island is not a good island; that Ralph must go on being chief; that, as chief, he must tell the others off when they fail to do the tasks of shelter-building and keeping the fire alight. More tellingly, he and Simon were at other rocks, early in Chapter 7. When **Simon told Ralph that he- Ralph- would get back all right,** Simon did not predict his own personal safety, or Piggy's; only Ralph's.

It seems to me that **it is this promise which makes Ralph unafraid of Jack, at least for now, and means he can disregard the strong visual terror which comes with the face-paint.**

We see that **Piggy and Ralph are united in their disability and loss of power; Piggy cannot see without his glasses, and Ralph cannot remember much of what he needs to, as a leader and decision-maker. They are now equals, helping and reassuring each other.**

The mission takes them back to where **Ralph** had gone on, alone, searching for the beast, in Chapter 6; now he is looking for, and **will face, a real beast, in the snarling, sneering creature Jack has become**. Ralph takes Piggy and the twins with him now, though he leads; he blows the conch and says he is calling an assembly, but the "savages" (they are no longer boys) do not respond because they only answer now to the fear-inducing call of Jack.

Just as Roger had thrown stones at the powerless Henry in Chapter 4, but had been inhibited by his cultural conditioning from aiming to hit him, so he throws a stone in the direction of the twins; only this time the same restraint does not hold him back.

Jack's appearance from the forest (with another dead sow) prompts the final, highly wrought confrontation between Ralph and him. Piggy is, again, pathetic, vulnerable, and a figure of fun. Jack responds to Ralph's accusation that he is a thief by lunging at him with his spear; their initial fight is not entirely serious, and belongs in the school playground.

He summons up a final passionate appeal about the need for a signal fire. Jack orders the- uncivilised- capture of the twins, knowing that Ralph will try to rescue them. Piggy demands to speak, and, in the silence, Roger is throwing stones near Ralph's head- with less and less restraint. **Piggy and Ralph present the baying crowd with the moral choice; is it "better" to hunt, kill and break society, or to have rules, agree actions and be rescued?**

But **Roger has** – not altogether deliberately, but not very accidentally- **released the great rock, which falls and knocks Piggy to his death. The sense of what Golding describes as "delirious abandonment" behind this act is the same as the fixation with the hunt which led Jack to break his promise about the fire in Chapter 2, and from which the clash of cultures has developed.**

Roger's manslaughter of Piggy unleashes the beast in Jack and the mob. Note here how the language is that of the pig-hunt, and how Ralph dodges the spears and runs into the forest as though he were a hunted pig. **The way in which Ralph is wounded and runs away reminds us of the hunt where Ralph wounded the boar in Chapter 7.** The beast does not distinguish between animals and people; it kills both, without conscience.

Jack scolds Roger for leaving his post and coming down to join the mob; he has done so because even he feels a sense of shock and guilt at killing Piggy.

Jack does not give it a moment's thought, but starts to hurt Sam by prodding him with a spear. Roger, the artist in residence for torture, steps forward to take over; there is an implied threat that the twins will be subjected to an extremely unpleasant initiation into this tribe, which they are being forced to join. The motiveless punishment of Wilfred in Chapter 10 has already stimulated Roger's instinct for testing the possibilities of what he may be able to do to helpless victims where there are no rules to hold him back.

It is an effective way to end a chapter, and **the reader (reading this just nine years after the end of World War 2) can't ignore comparisons with the Nazi concentration camps, the Japanese attitude to prisoners of war, and the possibility of experimental, unregulated torture by any regime.**

Chapter 12

All that is left now is **the final, unequal struggle between Jack, the hunter, and Ralph, the wounded, hunted animal.**

Removing the last of his allies, by allowing Piggy to be killed and the twins to be captured, enables Golding to

narrate the last part of the novel entirely from Ralph's feverish and desperate point of view.

Golding depicts Ralph as having the intelligence and the mind-set, now, of an animal, not a boy. When the twins tell him that Roger has prepared a stick sharpened at both ends, we remember the stake on which the sow's head was impaled, and left as an offering for the beast, and we understand that Jack and Roger mean to do the same to Ralph; but Ralph does not make the connection.

He realises that he has not been followed into the forest; Jack's tribe have pig to eat, and they are scared of the forest, because Jack has told them that the beast is still alive. He would like to think that he might be left alone to exist in solitude, excluded from Jack's tribe; but he knows that Jack's personal antagonism is such that he will not fail to pursue him to death, because Piggy and Simon are dead, which means that there are no rules against hunting and killing people as if they were a sub-species. Ralph knows he has no protection against Jack.

He comes across the sow's head in Simon's clearing; his perception is that it is malevolent, and mocking him, and he smashes the skull, which then lies in two separated halves. The Lord of the Flies had threatened to have fun with Simon, as a euphemism for having him killed; we sense that the same fate awaits Ralph now. He takes the sharpened stick, less to protect him from hunters than to protect him from the Lord of the Flies. It does not speak to him; it does not threaten him in the way it had threatened Simon, because, contrary to our fears, Ralph will survive and be rescued.

Ralph watches Jack's encampment, hoping against hope for an end to hostilities. When he sees that Sam and Eric are on sentry duty, he speaks to them, and they allude to the fact that

Roger has been allowed to initiate them by torture. They say, too that, **the next day, Jack and Roger will "do" Ralph**- a verbal reference to the prophetic threat the Lord of the Flies made to Simon at the end of Chapter 8, and then carried out.

Ralph tells the twins where he plans to hide; Sam throws him some meat, and they tell him about the cordon, the methodology of the hunt (it is **different from a pig-hunt, because it is a manhunt**). And they warn him that Roger has a sadistic plan for him, with his sharpened stick.

He hears the twins being hurt again; he does not realise it, but the secret he gave them- of where he would be hiding- has been extracted from them already.

The rock which knocked Piggy to his death had bounced into the forest, and created what Ralph thinks is a safe hideout. But Jack appears, coercing the twins to reveal the hiding place Ralph had told them about. He thinks he is still safe, because the undergrowth is impenetrable; but they roll a huge rock to clear it, and then an even bigger one, which does not bounce, but flattens the forest. **We are reminded both of the rock which killed Piggy and of the rock-rolling in more innocent and playful times, in Chapter 6, and, especially, in Chapter 1, when no-one had any intention of killing anyone else.**

In panic, Ralph wounds a nearby savage (a boy, in reality), and so gives away his location. **The tribe sets the forest on fire, to smoke him out into the open. This is a link with the fatal forest fire in Chapter 2 (where the small boy with the birthmark died) and with Ralph's insistence all the way through the novel that only a large fire with a lot of smoke will enable them to be rescued.**

**This fire immediately generates huge quantities of smoke-
but we do not think it will be a means of rescue, because
we feel so acutely the danger Ralph is in.**

Ralph attacks another savage/boy, like a cat, stabbing him, in
an attempt to escape. He rests, and tries to think what to do. As
he found so often in the assemblies, the need to make a wise
decision is compromised by a lack of time to think (see the
opening pages of Chapter 5).

Hiding up a tree is potentially dangerous- if you are seen, there
is no escape; and running through the human chain does not
guarantee more than a temporary freedom. He is behaving like
a horse; he tries to think of what a pig would do in this situation.

The forest undergrowth is burning. Ralph finds himself facing
the sow's broken skull again; he hides, much as Simon had
hidden in his solitary den in Chapters 3 and 8.

Even this hiding place is not safe, and the savage who finds
him is Roger, the sadist, because his weapon is a stick
sharpened at both ends. Golding brings him closer and closer
to Ralph, until Ralph is staring at him, and Ralph loses his
nerve, while he clings to the last shred of hope, which is
Simon's prediction that he will be rescued. He jumps, and runs
to the beach, only to find himself facing, not Jack or Roger, but
a uniformed Navy officer.

We see the boys now through the officer's eyes; they are small,
dirty, less dangerous. **Ralph says that two have been killed;**
in fact, there have been three deaths, so which of Simon, Piggy
and the boy with the birthmark has he forgotten about?

The arrival of an adult changes everything and how everyone
behaves. Percival cannot remember his own name and
address any longer. Ralph says that he *is* in charge of the boys

(when clearly only moments ago he was not); Jack thinks about challenging him, but does not.

The officer points out that, because they are British boys, they should at least know how many of them there are. Ralph is struck by the enormity of the pain he has gone through and the deaths of Simon and Piggy, whom he describes with accuracy as a "true, wise friend". For all the boys, **the age of innocence is over.** We hear it from Ralph, but it applies to most of these boys when he says that he has seen directly into "the darkness of man's heart". And, when he says man, he means every man and all society.

Characters and how they develop

Ralph

Ralph is the first character to appear, although he is referred to as the boy with the fair hair several times, before his name is revealed.

He is a few months past his twelfth birthday. Golding gives him some childish vocabulary and characteristics- he imitates a fighter plane, and has a habit of standing on his head. He cannot keep the secret of Piggy's name, and he is easily provoked to laughter, easily delighted; optimistic. His father is a commander in the Navy, who taught Ralph how to swim when he was five. He has an active imagination, tends to daydream, and thinks that the island is a place of fantasy and fun. Ralph tends to respond to new people with a shy friendliness. He is considerate, and moderately charismatic.

Ralph is chosen as the boys' leader for a number of reasons. One is the accident that he found the conch (with which he calls them to assemblies) - this sets him apart. But his appearance is attractive; his size makes him a candidate; and he has calmness, or a quality of stillness, which suggests a disciplined and methodical mind.

Within minutes of being chosen, he tells Piggy that he cannot go on the expedition to explore the island- he has grasped at once that a leader has to make decisions, some of which will not be popular. Ralph is the first boy to realise that a leader, or chief, is needed, and he is the only one (until Piggy understands this) who appreciates that maintaining a signal fire is vital if they are to be rescued.

He is not as ruthless as he needs to be. Although he has the physical makings of a boxer, his mouth and eyes express a natural mildness, and his fatal mistake, right at the beginning of his tenure as chief, is to allow Jack to keep the choir and designate them as hunters. This will feed Jack's obsession, so that Ralph will finally become the hunted prey of those who have usurped him- Jack and his sadistic colleague Roger.

Ralph challenges Jack to become a killer of pigs. He allows him his own army because he is keen to offer him some consolation for his disappointment that he was not chosen as chief.

Although Ralph is not arrogant, initially we may tend to interpret his excited declarations that the island now belongs to him and the other boys as such. The island rebels against this abuse by the boys who invade and occupy it. But as the book develops, Ralph is shown to respect the island. It is Jack who violates it.

In my view, Ralph is simply a confident British schoolboy, growing up in the 1950s when there is still a British

Commonwealth (and even an Empire) stretching around the world. He is certainly attached to the idea that people behave according to the rules; he is slow to understand the power of the methods of mob rule, of whipping up a crowd, which makes Jack more effective in getting people to do what he wants. Ralph thinks that the conch will guarantee order; it will not.

While Ralph is too trusting, he is good at providing reassurance. His confident statements- that the island is good, that the boys can have a good time, and that naturally, sooner or later, they will be rescued by ship- make the other boys feel better; and they like him and respect him. He speaks well and is an effective communicator. But he cannot remove the nightmares, the fear of the beast that the smaller boys have, because he is not in charge of the hunters; the challenge to provide a sense of security is beyond him, because he cannot create a sense of "society", or a group identity (like hunters or the choir, or a tribe of savages).

Ralph sees the big picture, but he is easily distracted from the supervising and attention to detail which is needed in order to make the rabble of boys (and especially the six-year-olds) useful and even safe. The small boy with the birthmark is unaccounted for – lost in the fire- in Chapter 2, and Simon dies partly because there is no system for knowing where he is.

Ralph's decision, at the first assembly, to explore the area, and see whether it is inhabited or not, and an island or not, is reasonable- but he does not leave instructions for anything useful to be done in his absence. In Chapter 2, the second decision- to make a fire- becomes chaotic, because it is disorganised; and, in chapter 3, we find Ralph trying to make the shelters, with Simon (who, acutely, observes that, as chief, Ralph should be telling off the boys who are doing nothing to help). Ralph is frustrated by how much talk and how little action there is, and he personalises this, pointing out to Jack that he has not yet killed a pig, or brought meat. This will just fuel the fire of Jack's irrational obsession with bloodshed. It fuels not friendship or collaboration (which they had managed when they made the fire) but antagonism.

One of the advantages of depicting a conflict between twelve-year-olds is that it is convincing for it to go unresolved; boys of this age do not have the verbal range or the negotiating skills to talk it through and resolve it.

Their very different interests are dramatized in Chapter 4; Ralph can see smoke from a ship's funnel on the horizon, but Jack has failed in his promise to have his hunters keep watch and maintain a fire (and Ralph has failed to keep them to that promise). Jack returns with his first kill, but Ralph confronts him with the facts that there was a ship (they could have been rescued), and he had let the fire burn out.

His disapproval puts an immovable barrier between Jack and him. Conflict, not cooperation and understanding, will be the defining quality of their relationship for the last two thirds of the novel; one post or job of chief, and two candidates. The chapter ends with Ralph announcing that he is calling another assembly- the third one we will have watched (though there have been more, omitted from the narrative). We assume that this will be designed to resolve the question of where decision-making authority lies- with him, or with Jack.

For Ralph, the initial pleasure and glamour of the adventure in an exotic fantasy world is wearing off- instead, he feels the physical discomfort of having hair that is too long, ill-fitting clothes, and no bed. He feels the burden of the responsibility for making decisions; the need for wisdom and thinking ability (which he now sees is a quality Piggy has).

He decides that fires can only be lit on the mountain; and he tries, again, to settle the question of what they are all, in their own ways, afraid of. It is Jack – again - who turns the abstract fear into a concrete object- the beast - and asserts that it has not been sighted, but that if it were, it would be hunted and killed- so there is nothing to fear. But two of the littluns (Phil and Percival) are not capable of being convinced of this; Simon offers the idea that the beast is "only us", and someone else suggests it is a ghost.

Ralph defines the going off at tangents, the ignoring of the central and overriding need for the fire, as "the breaking-up of sanity"; fear, as in, for example, a majority belief in the possibility of ghosts, is preventing logical, prioritised, meaningful self-help. The assembly dissolves into chaos; Ralph threatens to give up, but Simon and Piggy insist that he must continue, because the alternative, under Jack, is anarchy without any hope of rescue.

The next morning, the existence of the beast appears to be confirmed; Sam and Eric have seen it. Ralph had been dreaming of his life in Devon, feeding ponies. Just as at the beginning of the novel, there must be an expedition- this time, to hunt the beast and to reignite the fire on the mountain. Ralph must go; so will Jack, who is impulsive and mutinous, but still lacks popular support; and Simon- the same trio as before.

Ralph tries to conceal his own fear, but he is facing inner terrors because he knows that when they reach the unexplored end of the island he, as chief, will have to lead the way. There is no beast there; Ralph has to insist, again, on climbing the mountain, to eliminate the possibility that the beast is real, and to attend to the fire. That expedition goes ahead, in the dark, even without Piggy's glasses. It is no longer about the fire. It is a test of who is less brave- Ralph or Jack.

At the end of Chapter 6, Ralph experiences the first episode of mental disintegration, which takes the form of his being unable to put his ideas or thoughts into words. This will become a recurring theme. Golding uses it to sustain our empathy for Ralph under the pressure of trying to lead a rabble of boys whose behaviour is breaking down.

He has started to bite his nails (a sign of anxiety), and he no longer believes unambiguously that they will be rescued from the island. Ralph daydreams of his childhood in the winter snow, in a cottage, when "Mummy had still been with them" (an odd, unexplained reference; is she dead?) and the only terrors were imagined from book illustrations.

Caught up in the hunting of a wild boar, Ralph's excitement at his own aggression closes the gap between him and Jack; illogically, Ralph says he thinks that the escaped boar was the beast. Ralph had criticised Jack for hunting instead of helping to build shelters, when Jack could think only of the glamour and thrill of the hunt. Now he allows himself to be caught up in exactly the same kind of violent thrill, and he joins in the pantomime, jabbing at Robert (who plays the part of a boar) with Eric's spear.

Golding goes out of his way to show that Ralph, too, can behave like one of the mob- he feels an overwhelming desire to hurt (the helpless, defenceless pig). For him, the instinct to be violent is born from frustration and a growing sense of hopelessness; the safety of home seems to be receding.

The climb up the mountain, in fading light, leads to a confrontation; Ralph asks Jack why Jack hates him, and Jack insists on challenging Ralph's courage; he wants to undermine Ralph's authority and discredit him. Ralph accepts the challenge, and maintains his self-control. He is tired, worn out, so he lets Jack go forwards first from the ashes of the fire, while he waits with Roger. When Jack returns, shocked by what he has seen, Ralph is calm and resolute, insisting that they must all look. Jack and Roger both hang back. We see the dead parachutist as Ralph sees him, and the three boys run away in terror.

Ralph projects on to the beast the idea that it does not want the boys to be rescued; he is prepared to admit defeat. Jack calls an assembly, to accuse Ralph of being a coward and not a proper leader but Ralph still has the boys' support. After Jack has made his unsuccessful challenge, Ralph still feels defeatist, because the threat of the beast now makes keeping a fire on the mountain impossible; but he accepts Piggy's suggestion that they should make a fire on the beach (the choice Ralph had forbidden in Chapter 5- he is now breaking his own rule). He finds that his bitten nail is making his finger bleed. When we read this, we know that the outlook is not good - in this novel, shedding a little blood is a symbolic sign that the character concerned is about to endure a period of suffering.

In Chapter 8, Ralph confides in Piggy; the fact that the other boys do not accept the vital significance of the fire means that there is a chance they will all die here; their prospects are deteriorating. Ralph's view is endorsed by the thunderous atmosphere and the sudden theft of the fire by Jack, who is now a naked painted savage.

Ralph is losing the capacity to express himself; he is starting to need Piggy to prompt him to complete his sentences.

He can no longer maintain his authority, because Jack delivers meat to the boys and promises to protect them from the beast. He (and Piggy) are not quite detached from the charade of pig-killing, which turns into the killing of Simon.

Ralph knows that this was a murder; the escalating violence frightens him (because there is nothing to contain it, and because he and Piggy know that Jack hates them both). Piggy and the twins are reluctant to acknowledge the implications; they refer to the murder, euphemistically, as a "dance".

Where, throughout the first eight chapters, Ralph was seldom out of the reader's sight, his role in chapters 9-11 is smaller, because the power to lead and drive the action has passed to Jack.

Ralph's power of speech is fading; what he says is shorter and less compelling or convincing. He wishes he could think like an adult. His resources, his knowledge of the world are fading. The need for fire is now as much for comfort as for attracting a rescue. The fire is a metaphor for Ralph's own optimism and leadership; both are burning low, becoming feeble, and, when he needs to be passionate and convincing, Ralph forgets what he wants to say. Unable to influence events, he now resorts to dreams, and in particular a fantasy of being a child at home in Devon again.

In Chapter 10, Ralph and Piggy are like King Lear and the Fool in the storm in Shakespeare's tragedy "King Lear". Stripped of his authority by his evil daughters, Lear acquires wisdom and humility, and a new compassion for his fellow creatures, through their shared suffering and his own mental breakdown. Ralph's attitude towards Piggy has changed, from being sarcastic and teasing to being considerate and receptive. Just as Shakespeare uses eyesight symbolically (being able to see does not guarantee insight), Golding uses Piggy's glasses as a symbol of fire, power and hope. At the end of Chapter 10, they are broken and in Jack's possession.

Without fire, or the means to start one, Ralph is outraged by the theft of Piggy's glasses and their own fire; but he is handicapped because of his mental anguish. He is now unable to finish his speeches, and Piggy has to speak for him. Piggy shares his sense of offended morality, and they set out on the pathetic, doomed mission to ask for the glasses back.

The language of the confrontation between Ralph and Jack in Chapter 11 is that of the school playground; so is the fight itself. But Sam and Eric are captured, then the conch is shattered, and Piggy is killed; and Jack means to kill Ralph.

In Chapter 12, Ralph experiences the heightened fear of the hunted animal; he is involved in a desperate struggle to avoid capture by Jack and Roger, who, he knows, will kill him. He still hopes, fleetingly, that he can declare "pax", as though the hunt to the death is a game in the school playground; or that he will be left in peace, perhaps with Sam and Eric. For a split second, he tries to convince himself that Piggy's death was an accident.

Under stress, hungry and in a hopeless situation, he is angry with the Lord of the Flies. As he tries to evade capture, he is described as being like a horse, a cat, a pig. We feel the stress of being hunted, and how difficult it is to think clearly under that pressure.

Ralph tells the naval officer that two boys have been killed. He seems to have forgotten about the boy with the birthmark. This should be seen as a sign of how damaged Ralph's mind and memory have become; not of carelessness on the part of Golding!

Piggy

We hear Piggy before we see him; he emerges from the forest, backwards, fatly, and in his thick glasses. The next thing we notice about Piggy is his dialect and level of education. He speaks with a London/Essex accent and his grammar is often incorrect - for example, he may say "we was" when it should be "we were".

Piggy tries to befriend Ralph as an equal, but he is unsuccessful; Ralph does not ask him his name, and is unimpressed to find him following him about. When Piggy uses the forest as a toilet, grunting (like a pig), Ralph tries to escape from him- an odd inversion of all the pig-hunting later in the novel!

Piggy cannot swim, and his effort to make friends with Ralph extends to a confession of his nickname, and a careful undressing process which is quite painful for the reader. Piggy cannot do anything without pain (or effort), determination and concentration; nothing comes easily to him. He is contrasted with Ralph in every way; as well as his physical disadvantages, his father is dead, where Ralph's is a commander in the Navy. Instead of learning to swim (he was not allowed to, because of his asthma), Piggy has been spending his childhood eating an unlimited quantity of sweets.

However, Piggy appreciates, as Ralph does not, that the boys must do something, because their location is not known to any adults. He also knows how the conch can be blown; though he does not have the physical capacity to do it himself. He starts to refer to himself and Ralph as "we" and "us", but then encourages Ralph to take the credit for bringing the conch up out of the sand- Piggy is a facilitator, not a leader in his own right. He coaches Ralph until he blows the conch properly.

He feels intimidated by Jack's uniformed gang and his offhand authority- the natural, assumed social superiority of the public-schoolboy. Piggy's fear of Jack becomes more and more acute as the tale develops.

Piggy votes for Ralph as leader grudgingly- he is the last boy to raise his hand. Like Jack, but for very different reasons, Piggy would like to be leader himself; but it will never happen, because others cannot see beyond his physical disadvantages. He is disregarded, just because he does not look like a leader. But Jack, who has the swagger of a leader, is overlooked too; the reasons why Jack is not chosen are more complex, and they are to do with trust and being able to communicate with a wider audience.

Piggy tries to volunteer as the fourth member of the leadership/exploring group (with Ralph, Jack and Simon), and he hangs on to them, again, until Ralph tells him he must stay behind. He feels humiliated and hurt by Ralph's easy disclosure of his nickname, but he responds positively to being given the task of taking boys' names.

At the assembly in Chapter 2, he supports Ralph, makes his point that no one knows they are on the island, and encourages all the boys to respect the rule that the conch gives the right to speak to whoever is holding it (a belief he clings to, pathetically, as late as Chapter 11). He is scathing about the disorganised rush to go and make a fire (he says that they are acting like a crowd of kids, when of course that is what they are!), and Golding casts him here as a parent who has- reluctantly- to keep up with his energetic children.

He appears on the mountain, with the conch and his glasses, without which the fire could not be lit- he is pathetically terrified of handing his glasses over, and Golding continually returns to how helpless he is when he cannot see. This is a good way to make us empathise with Piggy (the boys in "The Coral Island" did not have glasses, and knew how to light fires!).

His criticism of the disorganised fire-making proves justified. He complains to Ralph that he is not listened to, where Jack, Maurice or Simon are; and that the small fire they wanted has set the island on fire. His complaint is that organisation must come first; shelters before fires, and democratic speaking. It is interesting that this becomes Ralph's recurring theme- it comes from Piggy first. With devastating impact and detachment, he points out that the small boy with the birthmark on his face is unaccounted for, and others, too, may have been burnt alive further down.

Piggy's scientific and analytical knowledge of the world means he knows about optical illusions and mirages and does not believe in ghosts or monsters. He is the only boy whose hair never grows, as though he is naturally bald (older? wiser?) unlike children of his own age. Ralph finds him dull and boring, but Piggy does not realise when he is being teased; he remains serious, purposeful and positive. He responds enthusiastically and appreciatively to anything he thinks is a sign of friendliness, because he is treated as an outsider- not just because of his physical disadvantages but because he is lazy.

Jack's unforgivable neglect of the fire leads (in Chapter 4) to Piggy replacing him as Ralph's right hand man; and, at the start of Chapter 5, Ralph understands that Piggy is smart. He stands outside the assembly, as a small, fairly pointless protest, but soon joins it. He says that there cannot be a beast in the forest and thus there is nothing to be afraid of, and he judges that being afraid is a medical condition of "the inside of your mind", so that the fear is real enough, but the beast does not have a physical existence.

Piggy wants to talk of the fear of people (because he is frightened of Jack) but he invites the smaller boys forward to explain their fear. The problem with this is that the irrational cannot be dealt with rationally; there is no reassurance for them; and the assembly threatens to break up in chaos.

First, there is a discussion about ghosts- Piggy states his own position (he does not believe in ghosts, and is emphatic about this), and when there is a vote which shows that the majority of the boys do, he shouts, shrilly, "I didn't vote for no ghosts!". He sees primitivism of this sort as belonging to animals or savages, not civilised people; he is right that the surrender of rationality is a quick route towards the savagery with which Jack (and Roger) rule the boys in the next chapters.

Piggy suggests, weakly, as a response to the twins' inaccurate description of the beast, that the boys could simply avoid it, and stay down on the beach. He is apprehensive, too, about being left to look after the smaller boys while all the others hunt the beast.

At the start of Chapter 8, Piggy hears Ralph's account of the beast (the parachutist), while he polishes his glasses (a sign that he is thinking). Jack's self-imposed exile gives Piggy new optimism of a life without Jack breathing down over him. Liberated from his fear of Jack, Piggy is more confident and creative. He suggests that the beast can be avoided by making fire on the beach; Ralph agrees. Piggy feels so involved now that he even fetches some wood; he no longer feels a bullied and mocked outsider. He lights the new fire himself.

He has noticed- before Ralph- that Maurice, Bill and Roger have all gone in the same direction as Jack. Piggy is aware, now, that he needs to raise the spirits of the others, because a leader should, and Ralph is tired of providing leadership. Piggy and the twins go to the forest to bring Ralph fruit for a (meat-free) feast. Piggy wants to convince Ralph that, even with fewer in their tribe, and with no meat to eat, they will prosper, keep a fire up, and be rescued.

Towards the end of chapter, Ralph confides his fears and worries to Piggy in a way he has not done before; Piggy's intellectual distinction virtually makes him the senior partner now. They are discussing Jack's destructive influence when he bursts on their camp to steal burning branches they can use for their own fire.

Piggy now has to prompt and remind Jack (who is losing the power to express his ideas) about the importance of rescue. He and Ralph both understand the seductive attraction of hunting, fun and tribalism which Jack intends to offer recruits to his camp; they agree to go to the feast/party. They pretend they are going to ensure nothing bad happens, but, really, they cannot stay away.

At the feast, Piggy realises, before Ralph does, that power has now passed to Jack, so that a confrontation is pointless. Piggy's instinctive aversion to conflict is a weakness as well as a strength, but at least, in Chapter 11, he will stand up for what is right, although that one is a fight he cannot win.

Piggy objects, at first, to Ralph calling Simon's death murder, and he tries to rationalise it as an accident, or something self-inflicted. Of all the boys, Piggy has most to gain from clinging to the protection of social norms, because he is a natural victim and a natural target for bullies. Calling Simon's killing murder is an admission that the power of law and order on the island has died, too.

Piggy is anxious that Ralph should not reveal to the twins that they had been present- he wants to preserve the illusion that the four of them live in a separate society which is still civilised and law-abiding.

In Chapter 10, he hears the attackers before Ralph does. Even Ralph is giving in to irrational fears about the beast. There is a rare moment of comedy when a voice whispers "Piggy", and even Piggy thinks that the beast has come! Then he suffers an asthma attack, as he always does at moments of stress. Piggy thinks that Jack and the others had come to take the conch; we know, before he does, that it was his glasses they wanted.

At the start of Chapter 11, Piggy insists that Ralph calls an assembly; Ralph puts the conch in Piggy's hands, and makes him speak first. Both boys express their opposition to what they describe as awful things (the murder of Simon) and the theft of fire and Piggy's glasses. Piggy is driven by the basic need to be able to see properly. He speaks of Simon's killing as murder, and intends to confront Jack peacefully, with the conch, to demand that he does what is "right". He intends to face his fear (of Jack), as Simon would require. The trouble is that this show of morality will carry no weight without physical force to back it up, because he is dealing with someone who now only understands physical force.

Piggy is now the leader, exposed to risk- Ralph has Simon's promise of his own personal safety to protect him, but Piggy, whose safety Simon did not guarantee, is to take the conch. He supports Ralph sensitively, as Ralph continues to lose his grasp and effectiveness. When they arrive at Castle Rock, Ralph leads the way; the non-swimming Piggy is (understandably) worried about falling into the sea. That is ironic, as he will soon be thrown fatally on to the rocks below.

Despite his fear and vulnerability, Piggy reminds Ralph of the reason they have come, and he insists on speaking, with the conch, to the hostile crowd. They boo and shout, and Roger releases the rock which knocks Piggy over and pushes him to his death. To the very end, Piggy is committed to the idea of the conch, of democracy, free speech, and the values and morals of the adult world.

Piggy's death is brutal and sudden- he has not even time to grunt- but he is the last boy mentioned, at the end of the novel- "the true, wise friend called Piggy".

Jack

Just as Ralph and Piggy were introduced obliquely, as the fair, then the fat boy, Jack is described as "the boy who controlled" the choir; at the end of the novel, he virtually controls the whole island (although his fire, like the fire in Chapter 2, threatens to destroy his tribe's survival, by burning their food supply).

Jack is dressed similarly to his black-cloaked and black-capped troops (who seem like Nazis, or the UK fascist Mosley's blackshirts- they are like black birds). Jack has more energy than these other boys, and a sense of his own superiority. When Simon faints, he shows no shred of concern, claiming his collapse is an act.

He seems dissatisfied with Ralph; he does not consider (here or anywhere else in the narrative) that anyone has a better claim to be "chief" than he does. He is described as being tall and bony, with an ugly face, red hair, freckles and a crumpled face. His eyes are light blue, and generally he is either angry or on the point of being angry.

He orders the choir, who have to ask him for rest; and they have to address him by his title- his surname- Merridew. He refuses to be called by his Christian name; he means to say that he disapproves of informality, or a democratic friendliness which assumes that everyone is equal.

Sensing Piggy's weakness, Jack reveals that he is a bully- he tells Piggy "shut up, fatty". Then he puts his (arrogant) case for his own leadership bid- before there has been any discussion at all. He is a chapter chorister as well as head boy, presumably at a prep-school, and he can sing C sharp.

None of these attributes is an entitlement. He underestimates the quiet opposition from the choir, who must know how tyrannical he would be if he had a bigger empire (the empire he acquires in the later part of the novel). Jack has no regard for democracy, or for approval; he has the drive of the tyrant/dictator. He protests at the very idea of a democratic vote. Although he is the most obvious leader, according to Golding- because of his presence- the crowd chooses Ralph, as someone they *want* to follow.

Even the choir applauds when Jack is not chosen (out of relief) - although they had felt obliged to vote for him. He blushes when he loses the contest with Ralph, and this defeat sets the scene for all of their subsequent confrontations.

He is quick to specify that the choir should be hunters; Ralph has made the mistake of appeasing him and making him, in effect, his potential successor. Jack smacks a sheath-knife into a tree-trunk- the first sign of his violent nature. At the end of Chapter 1, he cannot kill the piglet with this knife, because to kill is to break the taboo of civilised society. Jack makes face-saving excuses; he becomes fierce, defiant, and determined to be without mercy in future; and he slams the knife into a tree-trunk.

Chapter 2 opens with Jack showing signs of being fixated on pig-hunting; he is trying to grow into the role of meat-getter (just as Ralph is trying to grow into the role of leader). He threatens to hunt and kill any fear-inspiring snakes (which stem from the small boys' nightmares); later, it is the dual promise of providing meat and providing physical safety from the beast which enables him to usurp Ralph as chief.

The proposal that they must make a fire on the mountain sees Jack take the lead. He speaks to Piggy unpleasantly, using the key, humiliating word "fat" in a different context, (but so that Piggy will still feel its sting) when he says, "A fat lot you tried". He can never talk to Piggy without being rude and aggressive.

Although Jack likes the idea of punishing people who break the rules, he will disregard them when it suits him. In denying Piggy the right to speak, he says that the conch doesn't count on top of the mountain. Ironically, only a moment later, he is holding the conch, and speaking, claiming that the boys are not savages. In the light of the last two chapters of the novel, he could not be more wrong- especially about himself.

He promises to split his choir into two groups, one to hunt, and one to keep the fire going, and watch for ships.

At the start of Chapter 3, he is hunting, obsessively. He quarrels with Ralph over the relative importance of hunting and shelters; we are told that the hunters who should be watching for ships and tending the fire have been swimming instead, while Jack has been hunting on his own- another example of disorganisation, again, with very serious consequences, as the potential rescue ship sails past in the next chapter.

He is so obsessed with making a kill that he has almost forgotten about the issue of being rescued; he rams his spear into the ground, another expression of frustration. Ralph warns him- ironically, for the reader- about his promise to take responsibility for the fire, which Jack does not see as his overriding obligation.

Comically, Jack "sees", not the ship, but why he cannot find pigs- they hide in the shade in the hottest hours- and invents the idea of face-paint as a disguise; he puts this into practice in Chapter 4, where he shows Roger, who approves of the sinister principle of deceiving your prey.

Jack is careful to test the face paint in front of other boys, to be sure it is frightening (not in front of Ralph and Piggy, though); he wants his plan for successful hunting to be effective, so it must be cunning. He is pleased to find that he has turned himself into "an awesome stranger". The anonymity the paint gives him turns his laughter into a snarl.

Golding tells us that dressing like this destroys in him any sense of "shame and self-consciousness". Removing civilised conventions- of being visible and accountable- frees him to be his natural, unpleasant self. His tribe are almost all painted, so that they can be violent without being answerable for their violence.

In Chapter 4, Jack makes his first kill. He does not like having blood on his hands, and wipes it on his shorts - he is not yet completely comfortable shedding blood (this will change soon enough). But he is laughing, grinning, dancing, happy- with his sense of achievement. We know, though he does not, that his glee will be cut short when Ralph explains that his neglect of the fire has let a rescue opportunity pass.

Golding tells us that the act of the kill has given Jack "knowledge" which is now in his memory; the knowledge that killing is not so difficult after all, and is actually a pleasure.

Confronted with the fact that he has let the others down, Jack is embarrassed. When Piggy weighs in with supporting criticism, he becomes violent and punches Piggy in the stomach, before calling him "fatty" again, in a vicious tone. Then he smacks Piggy's head, so that his glasses fall off and one lens breaks, and he mimics Piggy's distress and scramble to retrieve these glasses. These cruel antics raise the hunters to "a gale of hysteria" (surely a reference to the effect of Hitler's oratory during his rise to power).

Jack apologises for letting the fire go out; but he does not apologise to Piggy for breaking his glasses. He also feels angry and alienated from Ralph, "without knowing why". He should sense that the "link" between him and Ralph (of trust) is broken, and that Ralph will now take advice from Piggy rather than him. Perhaps this is why, when Piggy asks for meat, Jack wants to humiliate him all over again; he hunts Piggy as relentlessly as any other pig.

Jack tries to create a scene. His obsessive preoccupation with hunting has harmed them but he feels he must not lose face over it; so his embarrassment has to be kept to himself. He will not let the other boys relate the story of the kill, and his excited account makes the hunters dance and sing and chant.

In the assembly at the start of Chapter 5, Jack calls the littluns cry-babies because of their nightmares about a beast in the forest. He says that the hunters talk about the existence of an animal, but, having been all over the island, by himself, he does not think there is such a creature. Later in the assembly, when he shakes Percival, in an attempt to find out where the beast lives, he just collapses (perhaps from fright).

As the speculation about the beast continues, first Maurice undermines Jack's claim that there is no beast (there could be one), and then Simon suggests that the beast may exist, but it may be "only us". Jack drowns this out, by providing a word of "one expressive syllable" to describe "the dirtiest thing there is". I will do the same as Golding, and leave it to your imagination to supply the missing word!

This is a form of verbal violence; again, it is a crowd-pleasing gesture, which leaves the hunters screaming with delight.

Jack is angry, so he shouts at Piggy again, and again he calls him "Fatty". He tries to deny Piggy the right to speak. Then he challenges Ralph directly; Ralph can't hunt and he can't sing, gives orders that don't make any sense, and always favours Piggy. Jack now rejects the rules, and the assembly breaks up.

Piggy urges Ralph to blow the conch again, but he will not; Piggy says that if Jack were allowed to be leader, he fears what Jack would do to him; because he hates Piggy, he would hurt him (much later, Ralph asks Jack the same question; why does he hate him?). Piggy has already provided the answer. Jack hates Ralph because of his shame over the fire, and because Ralph is chief and he is not. Simon backs up the truth of what Piggy says.

The twins' account of the beast- like some monster in a Hollywood film- gives Jack the chance to swagger, to sneer at Ralph, and to challenge him to prove that he is not frightened. His rebelliousness continues to grow; again, he accuses Ralph, sarcastically, of wanting to keep Piggy out of danger, and says that some people should be excluded from making decisions (or speaking). This is a direct attack on the principle of democracy; it says that some people (he means, mainly, him) are better than others. He confronts Ralph, but Ralph outwits him, by reminding the boys that the issue here is not just hunting the beast, but relighting the fire.

Jack allows Ralph, as chief, to go forward to seek the beast on the unexplored part of the island, but he then follows him, and he sees the landscape as ideal for a fort (which he will set up soon- unknown to him, or Ralph, or the reader, at this stage). Ralph's insistence on the need for fire cannot keep Jack from going off to lead a rock-rolling party; after a near-mutiny, they resume the trek, and Jack, again, leads the way.

Chapter 7 sees the journey to the mountain incorporate another unsuccessful hunt; Ralph wounds the boar, the boar wounds Jack, and the boys act the hunt out immediately afterwards. Here, Robert plays the part of the boar; Jack has him by the hair, pulls a knife on him, Robert is hurt, and Jack says that, for realism, they need someone dressed as a pig- or they could use a small boy. In fact, he and Roger go on to hunt Piggy and Ralph.

Jack tries again to make an issue out of what makes him jealous- the preference he thinks Ralph has for Piggy. He sneers at Ralph, challenging him to prove his bravery, because his resentment always asserts itself as soon as he is not acting as leader.

When Ralph asks him directly *why* Jack hates him, Jack hangs back. He forces Ralph to go with him up the mountain. Physically and emotionally exhausted, Ralph lets Jack go first this time- a weakness which Jack tries to exploit (without success). He comes back aghast at seeing the dead parachutist, and, for the first time, Ralph finds him hesitant. He cannot face the sight a second time, and lags behind, while Ralph and Roger move towards the parachutist. He challenges Ralph with the telling question "Scared?", but he himself "slid away".

At the beginning of Chapter 8, Jack calls an assembly himself, for the first time, blowing the conch. The trigger for this is Ralph's frustrated labelling of the hunters as boys armed with sticks- powerless to fight the beast- but Jack has been building up to the moment where he would challenge Ralph openly as leader- and this is that moment. He hurries past his (now broken) promises that there is no beast in the forest, but if there were, he would kill it.

He airs his grievances about Ralph and what a poor leader he has been. The reader isn't worried about the outcome; we have seen the truth, and we know that the boys will have seen the same. The silence speaks volumes; Jack is shamed again, as he had been over the fire, and he announces that he is going into exile, and withdrawing his hunting service.

He announces to the tattered and degraded choir that he is going to be chief anyhow; and that they are no longer going to bother about the beast. There is a new chant; instead of "kill the pig" it is, almost, "forget the beast, and give a feast". Instead of hunting the beast, he plans to appease the beast by leaving "some of the kill for it".

Jack now has the confidence and skill to make an easy and repulsive kill of the sow. The ritualistic and primitive elements of the hunt are all Golding's; they are quite foreign to Ballantyne's "the Coral Island". The hunt is narrated partly from the sow's (personified) point of view; it becomes an execution at the hands of Jack and Roger. This time, Jack wipes the blood over Maurice's face and on a rock, not on his own shorts. He plans to use the meat to steal away boys who are still in Ralph's camp, and to steal their fire.

He tells Roger to "sharpen a stick at both ends" so that they can impale the sow's head and leave it for the beast; then they run shamefully away. This phrase foreshadows how Roger and Jack intend to treat Ralph when they have hunted him down in Chapter 12.

By the time of the raid on Ralph's camp for fire in Chapter 8, Jack has discarded his clothes- he wears just face and body paint and a belt. The idea of wearing cloaks and uniforms has been lost in the urge to become a savage. Jack has introduced the ritualistic (and faintly ridiculous) rule that, after he has made his speech, his henchmen- Maurice and Robert- must chant, together, the mantra "the chief has spoken".

Once he has meat and fire, Jack is all-powerful, and he creates a cult of himself (like Hitler or Stalin). He behaves like the tribal chiefs in "The Coral Island", painted and garlanded and issuing instructions; those chiefs are amoral, primitively superstitious and cannibalistic.

We can see now how Golding has dramatized the issue of evil by putting it within the group, whereas Ballantyne bolted it on from outside his trio of boys. Jack's "authority sat on his shoulder and chattered in his ear like an ape"- it is unevolved, over-excited, sub-human. He asks who wants "to join my tribe and have fun"; unidentified boys volunteer. Piggy and Ralph are isolated, and Ralph has lost the power to influence the group.

Jack promises to protect the boys from the beast, but he has no interest in providing shelters or in escaping from the island. His motive for leading is not the greater good of the boys, but his own sense of his own status. The lack of shelters, as the thunderstorm breaks, prompts the manic ritualistic dancing and chanting which create the context for killing Simon.

Up to the killing of Simon, Jack has been called Jack. Now, in Chapter 10, the narrative refers to him as "The Chief"- which is the title he has given himself. He gesticulates with his spear, and has "a bleak, painted face". He says that Simon was the beast, disguised, and that killing Simon has not killed the beast, which may come again. Jack no longer offers to lead a hunting party to kill the beast, because, now that he has complete control and power, he can simply maintain his power by intimidating his tribe. He will settle the last weakness- their lack of the means to light a fire- by raiding Ralph's camp again and taking Piggy's glasses.

When Ralph comes to try to take Piggy's glasses back, Jack is only recognisable by his red hair and personality   because he is also covered in black and green paint. When Ralph calls him a thief, he attacks him, but it is a play fight at first.

Jack orders the twins to be siezed, because he knows that Ralph will try to rescue them, and will be vulnerable. Now they have a serious, fierce fight, which Piggy interrupts, while Roger throws stones very near Ralph. When he feels he may lose the argument over what is right and what is wrong, Jack simply incites mob violence to drown Piggy out, and Roger drops the rock- the equivalent of the decisive nuclear or atom bomb.

Jack does not apologise for Piggy's sudden death; he attacks Ralph viciously, and tries to kill him. His battle for supremacy has become, literally, a matter of life and death. Again, once

Jack has wounded Ralph, the narrative refers to him as "The Chief". He does not chase Ralph into the forest, but stops beside the dead, hunted pig (a reminder of the dead, hunted Piggy). He intends to torment the twins mildly, but yields to Roger, who wants to torture them properly, and so almost pushes Jack out of the way. Jack appears to be in charge, but Roger's sadism has an authority of its own.

Simon

We meet Simon as he faints, face down, on the sand; we can only presume that he is particularly vulnerable to the tropical heat. The other choir boys put him into a recovery position and leave him be. When he recovers from fainting he gives his name. Golding does this with indirect speech; Simon does not speak to the reader yet.

Ralph chooses him to go with him and Jack on the mission to find out whether they are on an (uninhabited) island. Golding describes him as skinny and vivid with coarse, black, straight hair which forms a "hut". He identifies strongly scented green buds on an evergreen bush (which don't interest Ralph or Jack) as being like candles; symbolically, Simon sees light where others do not. He is the only boy who sees the parachutist for what it is.

He stands up to Jack, defending Piggy's contribution to the fire. He helps Ralph to build the third shelter, when no one else will, and tells Ralph to use his authority as chief to tell off the boys who are failing to help. When Ralph and Jack discuss the smaller boys' nightmares, Simon observes that they are talking and screaming "as if it wasn't a good island"- which is what he will be told by the Lord of the Flies in Chapter 8. (This makes sense, of course, but it is Simon's inner consciousness that "speaks" to him in the voice of the Lord of the Flies/the pig's head – because a dead pig's head cannot speak!)

In his absence, Ralph describes him as odd. He is shown to be kind in his habit of providing the best fruit from the higher branches for the small boys; then he goes on a faint path into the forest above, where he hides, and listens to the sounds of the island. The candle buds open here as nightfall comes on. We are left to work out for ourselves why Simon wants to be alone.

The way Golding presents him in Chapter 4 is striking. When the passing ship appears on the horizon, he stands next to Ralph, but is silent initially; then he cries out, as if he is hurt; he makes a timid attempt to touch Ralph, in a comforting way; then as he runs up the mountain with Ralph, to the fire, his face becomes twisted with anguish and when he realises that they will not be rescued this time, he turns away crying. When Ralph sees Jack in the distance, with his hunting procession, Simon appears to be afraid. He silences Piggy's snivel with a hush, as they wait for Ralph to confront Jack. All this time, Simon has no words at all.

Jack breaks Piggy's glasses, and Simon jumps on to the rocks to retrieve them. In an odd narrative phrase, Golding says that "passions beat about Simon on the mountain-top with awful wings". It seems that violence or confrontations cause Simon pain. When Jack makes a fuss over providing meat for Piggy, Simon hands Piggy his own (although he feels shame; perhaps he is disappointed at Jack's appalling attitude); it is another example of how he protects the vulnerable.

In Chapter 5, it seems possible that it is Simon going into the forest at night- on his own- who may have looked like a beast to the smaller boys, in the dark. He cannot explain in any detail why he was doing this; Ralph tells him not to do it again.

As the assembly dissolves, in speculation about a sea-borne beast, Simon takes the conch; although he hates speaking to any gathering, he feels compelled to do so. When he finally speaks, what he says is vitally important- "maybe, maybe there is a beast"- the reaction is a savage crying out- but "maybe it's only us". He is trying to express what Golding describes as "mankind's essential illness"- the capacity for savagery to our own species- but Jack drowns him out. Simon shrinks away because he is laughed out by the boys.

Simon is Golding's truth-teller- he knows what is wrong with people, and he both pities them and recoils from their bad behaviour.

At the end of Chapter 5, when Ralph wants to give up being chief, Piggy points out the risk of violent anarchy if Jack were to take over (all their time would be given over to hunting and the fire would go out). Simon speaks up in the dark, to give Ralph a simple instruction to go on being chief. He endorses what Piggy says about Jack's desire to hurt his enemies, and he repeats himself, for effect, that the only alternative chief is Jack, so Ralph must go on being chief to prevent that.

He has no time for the other two boys' escapist wishes; Ralph must keep the fire going. *That is a literal fire, but it is also the symbolic fire of civilisation against the forces of anarchy and tyranny.*

Simon recognises that the twins' description of the beast cannot be believed in. He knows that the beast is really a human being. The boys, as a group, experience or imagine the beast as an externalisation of their fear. They are all trying to be brave (remember, they are small boys – the oldest are only in Year 7), but they are rendered ill (remember Piggy's idea of an afflicted mind) by their fears and weakness.

Simon walks alongside Ralph, but a spot on his face starts to bleed when he bumps into a tree. This is a sign that he is about to undergo suffering. When Ralph has to take on the search, as leader, although he is a 12-year-old (not a mythical monster-slaying hero like Beowulf), Simon tries to reassure him, and lessen his fear, by saying he doesn't believe there is a beast out there anyway.

Chapter 7 sees Simon maintaining this role as Ralph's guide and mentor, when he faces difficulties which he lacks the confidence to confront. Now, Simon tells him the outcome will be rescue, after all- even if not for Simon himself. He states the same message three times, for effect, and they understand each other.

Because he has no fear of the beast, and no fears for himself, Simon goes, alone, to tell Piggy the hunting party will not be back at the beach until after dark.

In Chapter 8, after Ralph and Jack have confirmed that the beast is real, Simon takes the conch and suggests that they should all climb up the mountain. He answers Piggy's question of why should they, with another of his own- "What else is there to do?". He means that the only thing worth doing is to face our fears and confirm the truth for ourselves; something Piggy will not do. After saying this, Simon goes as far away from the group as he can.

He is missed, later in this chapter, but by this time he has gone back to his private retreat in the forest (the same place as at the end of chapter 3). Again, he sweats profusely in the oppressive heat. Dehydrated, he finds himself looking at the sow's head from Jack's brutal kill. Golding writes, opaquely, about Simon's "ancient, inescapable recognition" when he looks at the pig- presumably, the knowledge that animals and humans are connected by the violence with which we kill both.

At the end of Chapter 8 the Lord of the Flies calls Simon "a silly little boy…ignorant" and it describes itself as the Beast. The reader knows that Simon is neither silly nor ignorant; he is wise and serious. But the remarks seem to be directed less at Simon than at the boys as a group.

The important message here is that the Beast is "part of you"; then there is the threat to Simon, "you'll…….meet me down there……you're not wanted…..we shall do you". This threat seems cruel and unjustified, because Simon is completely innocent; but perhaps the point is to single out the least deserving for the most brutal treatment.

Golding is careful to include Piggy and Ralph in the list of names- the group which will "do" Simon. (Later, Roger will "do" Piggy and try to "do" Ralph). Simon has a fit, which leaves him with a burst blood vessel and blood around his mouth and chin. This turns out to be an unfortunate way to appear to the mob on the beach. We have a sense that something tragic is going to happen because of Golding's thematic use of blood to indicate violence, and because Simon's eyes have lost their usual brightness.

He repeats, out loud, his reason for going up the mountain, which he gave in exactly the same words in the previous chapter ("What else is there to do?"). The clear message is: we need to confront, directly, whatever we are afraid of. Where the other boys have been terrified of the dead parachutist, Simon is horrified, but compassionate, so he releases the corpse from the tangle it is in.

Simon's insight- that perhaps the beast is only us- has been confirmed; what the other boys think of as the beast is both harmless and horrible, yet should not give them nightmares. He wants to share this new knowledge with them at once. But the Lord of the Flies has warned him that he faces trouble on the beach, because he is not wanted- but is this not wanted by the island, or not wanted by the other boys (because of his maturity and understanding)?

Simon comes crawling and stumbling out of the forest. He is unrecognisable as a boy. The "teeth and claws" that Golding refers to here, actually belong to the mob (not to Simon, certainly) - and not, as the twins had described, to the beast in the forest, because the beast is not in the forest; it is wherever the boys gather.

Roger

Look carefully at the initial description of Roger. He is an outsider, secretive, and unwilling to talk. When Jack expects to be appointed leader without a contest, he says, simply, they should have a vote. He is a rebellious, pessimistic, dark-souled loner.

In Chapter 2, he says that he has already been watching the sea and he thinks, contrary to the group's confident optimism, that perhaps they will never be rescued. In Chapter 4, he kicks over the sandcastles built by Percival, Henry and Johnny, for no reason. He seems to have kept out of the sun, and has gone beyond being simply unsociable and remote to become forbidding. Potentially dangerous coconuts fall from trees sixty feet above him, but he is untouched, physically and emotionally. He throws stones at Henry, aiming to miss him narrowly, for his own entertainment. When he throws missiles at Piggy and Ralph in Chapter 11, he aims to hit, because there is no one to deter him. He enjoys keeping out of Henry's sight; he likes to be the anonymous, invisible torturer. Jack sees him, but not his vicious behaviour; he chooses Roger to try the face painting with.

Roger volunteers to go up the mountain with Ralph and Jack in Chapter 7, to hunt for the beast and relight the fire. *Whenever there is the possibility of a serious fight, he wants to be there.* He sits on a log next to Ralph, but says nothing. He just taps his spear against something on the mountain; he is beyond the reach of normal human contact.

He makes a joke of Jack's distress and shock over seeing the beast; he says that something that bulges must be a frog. Even his bravado fails him; he lags behind Ralph and Jack.

In the pantomime of pig-killing on the beach, which provokes Simon's death, at the end of Chapter 9, Roger acts the part of the pig, but not for long; he soon changes to a hunter, and leaves a gap which requires a victim to fill it.

At Castle Rock, in Chapter 10, Roger admires the rock which is poised to drop on attackers, and is controlled by a lever. He hears that Wilfred is going to be beaten (publicly) for no apparent reason (really, just to make an example of someone, because Jack depends on ruling by fear), and is being held tied up for hours. <u>A community where he can inflict cruelty on victims without punishment or accountability suits Roger perfectly</u>.

When Ralph, Piggy and the twins arrive in Chapter 11, and Jack is in the forest, Roger seems to be in charge of the aggressive defence of Castle Rock. He throws a stone between the twins, aiming to miss; Sam nearly slips. Then he throws stones near Ralph, and with a sense of abandonment. It is power without responsibility he craves- so he releases the rock which kills Piggy.

He comes down from his lookout post with "the hangman's horror"- an ambiguous phrase, which seems more likely to mean that others are frightened of him than that he feels he has done the wrong thing. This gives him the chance to take on the role of torturer of the twins.

Roger turns his attention to the hunt for Ralph by sharpening a stick at both ends. This implies that he intends to decapitate Ralph and leave his head on the stick for the beast. Ralph understands, in Chapter 12, that Roger is out to kill him. It is his final face to face encounter with Roger- eyeball to eyeball- which leads him to break cover and make his final despairing run for the beach.

Sam and Eric

I do not admire Golding's treatment of the twin boys. He treats the existence of twins as an eccentricity of Nature; Sam and

Eric grin and pant like dogs. Everything they do- even breathing and grinning- they do together. Golding also says that they seem to have insufficient skin for two and they are open-mouthed. This is nonsense. They are like a circus act, apparently; when Piggy confuses their identity, they shake their heads and point at each other and the other boys all laugh.

The twins pull a log, to help make the fire on the mountain, and when they realise that dry leaves are needed too, Golding calls this "unsuspected intelligence"- as though twins somehow have to share a single intellect. In Chapter 5, Golding says that they share "one wide, ecstatic grin".

They object to Jack's war paint in Chapter 4, but he waves them away, and sends them to bring him a coconut which he can fill with water and use as a make-up mirror. They do not want to join in the Jack's mime of pig-hunting, but, against their conscious will, and in fear, they do.

When Jack celebrates his first hunting kill, in Chapter 4, the twins are carrying the stake from which the pig is swinging, with its head hanging down. They should have been minding the fire, but Jack insisted that he needed them to do this instead. When Jack tells the story of the hunt, Golding repeats again that they have one identical grin between them as they jump and run about together.

They next appear at the start of Chapter 6, where they are minding the fire. They have both been asleep because they could never act independently. Although Eric sees the dead parachutist first, Golding, as usual, resorts to caricature- they are "gripped in each other's arms, four unwinking eyes aimed and two mouths open". Predictably, when they run away, it is as if they had a single mind, not two minds.Their account to Ralph, Piggy and Simon is full of the awful unknown and menace as they hold on to each other. They tell the assembly that the beast is furry, with wings and claws, and that it slinks and followed them.

The twins are especially tempted by Jack's offer of a feast with meat in Chapter 8. Even so, they stay loyal, and they are still dragging logs for firewood in Chapter 10. With Piggy and Ralph, they sense that Simon's murder was gravely offensive, but they, too, find it difficult to acknowledge, because they were connected with it, by being at the meat-eating feast.

They still try to keep the fire going, despite their exhaustion. They agree to go on the expedition to retrieve Piggy's glasses, even though they are especially frightened by the war-paint, and they can tell that Ralph is on the verge of a breakdown. Their own resolve is being tested- they question the point of carrying on- but they remain stubbornly committed to what is right, until they are captured and tortured. When Jack captures them, they protest but are powerless.

After they are tortured (by Roger) they are sent to be lookouts, in Chapter 12. Ralph judges that they are savages like the rest, but they explain, by completing each other's sentences- another tiresome piece of characterisation on Golding's part- that they have been tortured and forced to change sides. They tell Ralph that Jack and Roger will "do" him (the same threat the Lord of the Flies made to Simon) and hunt him like a pig, but across the whole of the island. Sam gives Ralph meat; then they part and, from a distance, a short while later, Ralph hears them boys scream again as they are tortured some more. The next morning, they have been made to reveal Ralph's hiding place to Jack and Roger, which guides the course of the rocks they roll, to force him out into the open.

Maurice

Maurice is one of the choir, and physically the largest of them except Jack. He points out how green branches are needed, to produce a smoking fire. In Chapter 4, he is Roger's sidekick in destroying the smaller boys' sandcastles; he has been punished for bullying before, and is half-hearted about being a vandal here, because he is still under the influence of civilised manners.

He defuses the scene at the end of Chapter 4 when he asks Jack where he found the pig; the tension subsides, for the time being. He pretends to be the pig, in the hunters' circle. The word "pretended" is repeated; it is a direct contrast to when Simon is in the circle, in Chapter 9 and there is no pretending.

Maurice points out, in Chapter 5, that the beast could be a sea creature, because they haven't found all the animals in the sea yet; he takes the conch, and makes the distinction that Jack may be right to say there is no creature on the island bigger than a pig, but he cannot guarantee it. The non-existence of the beast cannot be proved. He is a rationalist, like Piggy.

He volunteers to go with Jack and Roger to steal the means to light the fire (Piggy's glasses), but he is worried that, in walking along the beach, after Simon has been killed, they may meet the beast again. He, like the other boys, has had to set aside his rational thoughts in order to belong to Jack's (mindless) group.

Percival

Percival Wemys Madison, of the Vicarage, Harcourt St Anthony, Hants appears at two key moments. First, he has the end of Chapter 5 to himself; there, Golding describes his terror in a way I find unconvincing and rather mannered. Second, he tries to identify himself to the rescuing officer, at the very end of the novel, but he cannot remember his own name, let alone his address- because the old world seems so nearly forgotten.

Percival has been introduced to us, in Chapter 4, as one of the two smallest of all the boys. He has already spent two days in a shelter, having what we might call a nervous breakdown. He cries when Maurice throws sand in his eye, and he cries again when Henry throws sand generally.

At the assembly in Chapter 5, Percival stands up, gives his name and address, and simply starts crying, which almost incites a hysterical sadness among the whole crowd. He gives wordless expression to the terrors felt by the small boys and expressed in words- just before Percival's wordless, whimpering dirge- by another small boy, Phil, whose fear of the beast is rationalised by the older boys as a nightmare. Some psychologists would say that this is the outlet for a repressed experience, so that we should not dismiss the possible reality of something just because it is in a dream.

When an author chooses names and addresses, it always raises the question of whether they have any special significance (we have already seen that, in using the names Jack and Ralph, Golding is making a connection with RM Ballantyne's "The Coral Island").

I cannot find a village called Harcourt St Anthony. But Saint Anthony of Padua is the patron saint of finding lost things or people. There is a village in Oxfordshire called Stanton Harcourt, where a prehistoric stone monument called "the devil's quoits" was overlaid by a RAF airstrip in the Second World War, and re-excavated in the early 1950s. **The name "Lord of the Flies" is a translation of "Beelzebub"- a name for the devil;** and here we have the devil's quoits and the patron saint of the lost (boys). It is interesting that Percival's address includes three elements- the Vicarage (Christian morality, middle class respectability, restraint, right and wrong); Stanton Harcourt (associated with the devil and with warplanes); and St Anthony- under whose influence, presumably, Percival will find his lost identity once he has left the island, with all the other lost boys who are rescued. One of the vicars at Stanton Harcourt (who occupied the vicarage) was William *Percival* Walsh (1845-1911).

"Harcourt *St Anthony*" is strangely similar to "Stanton Harcourt". I can't help wondering whether Golding is playing a little game with names, to stress that the primitive and the violent are everywhere- even in rural Oxfordshire, which you might think is the classic definition of a civilised England.

In Chapter 5, Jack, who is interrogating him about the whereabouts of the beast, shakes him, and he collapses. But he starts the new rumour that it comes out of the sea. That small comment gives the beast a new dimension of terror.

Johnny

He is the first of the littluns to emerge from the forest when Ralph blows the conch in Chapter 1. Johnny is presented as a glorified toddler, with his trousers falling down; he sucks his thumb; but he is about six.

Golding refers to him as "innocent". In showing him as younger than his (already young) age, he stretches this concept to its limits. The end of the novel is also "the end of innocence" for the boys. They have seen for themselves how easy it is to become hunters and killers, where there are no grown-ups to make rules and make the rules be followed.

Key themes and ideas

After reading this far, you will have your own sense of what Golding's story is really about. See whether you agree with this suggestion-

Golding is interested in where violence comes from; in how we can manage conflict; and in how the world can be made a safer place.

The issue of **violence** is on almost every page of the novel. Jack and Roger become extremely violent and bloodthirsty, the longer they are on the island. Even Ralph and Piggy join in, to some extent, when Simon is murdered. Violent nightmares fuel the concept of the beast. What we might think of as a peaceful, tranquil island turns out to be dangerous and life-threatening.

Golding does not present everyone as equally violent (Jack is doing violent things from the start), but he does present violence as a form of madness, and he presents it in different forms. Jack uses violence (public beatings, and torture) to frighten his tribe into continuing to obey him. His leadership seems to offer no other purpose than reinforcing his power and attacking whoever he sees as his enemy.

The clearest examples of real leaders of this type are Hitler (Germany) and Stalin (Russia).

Hitler's belief in the innate supremacy and purity of the Germanic people resulted in the persecution of the (defenceless) Jews, which started with a notorious co-ordinated attack on Jews and their property, in November 1938. It was known as "Kristallnacht" (the night of the broken glass), because shops owned by Jews were vandalised, and was the first step in the increasingly evil persecution which became the Holocaust. Jack's vandalism of Piggy's glasses involves broken glass, and Jack steals the glasses later- just as the Nazis stole the property of Jewish people. Piggy is hunted to death, out of Jack's sheer, unjustified hatred; Hitler's concentration camps make an instructive comparison.

Jack is like Hitler in the way he terrorises his tribe. Josef Stalin, who died in 1953, had been the tyrannical leader of Russia since 1941. He had a pact with Hitler (rather like Jack's co-operation with Roger); he had his enemies killed, including millions of his own people, and committed atrocities against Poland and its army. Hitler's invasion of Russia in 1941 made Stalin an unlikely ally of Britain and the USA, and, because Russia was on the winning side, a Soviet "bloc", including East Germany, and protected by a nuclear capacity, became a new geo-political beast from 1945 onwards.

If Jack and Roger symbolise these brutally repressive forces of cultish leadership, Ralph must be a symbol for the reasoned and reluctant aggression of the British. Perhaps Ralph's mistake, in letting Jack retain his hunters (and his self-importance) is a symbol of Neville Chamberlain's appeasement of Hitler. Then, Ralph's despair at the lack of support from the other boys would stand for Britain's isolation against Hitler until the USA entered the war after the Japanese attack on Pearl Harbour.

Golding takes care to make his allegory less specific than this. Hitler was epileptic; the fits, in "Lord of the Flies", are Simon's, not Jack's. Ralph and Jack are both English schoolboys; Golding is interested in- and dubious about- the idea that being British means that you will never feel the instinct to behave savagely. The naval officer who rescues the boys and ends the war amongst them is British, not American.

However, Jack's style of personality-driven, ruthless, fear-driven leadership is, broadly, that of Hitler, Stalin and what Golding refers to as "the reds". Ralph's milder, more democratic leadership style is Anglo-American.

Golding's novel was published almost a decade after the end of the Second World War in 1945. By then, the USA and Russia were superpowers with different ideologies (capitalist and communist). If Ralph and Jack symbolise Britain/USA and Russia respectively- allies in the war, but opposed to each other at either end of the island in the later chapters- then Golding seems to project the consequences of the triumph of communism as the regime of Jack. Jack has no ideological or political agenda, but the argument seems to be that the silent majority (of liittluns), who take no interest in who governs them or what they do, may be sleepwalking into a world where a Jack is in charge. And the consequences of that – which we see on the island – are catastrophic.

Once again, the allegorical meaning cannot be tied down to the history of the Cold War in the 1950s. Ralph wishes to end the game of being hunted, and to be accepted by Jack, or to be allowed to live in peace, perhaps with Sam and Eric; the imbalance of power Golding gives us, in Jack's favour, does not reflect the tense but equal balance between Russia and the West.

In the real world, adults would- perhaps- be capable of recognising and tolerating their differences, and co-existing, with different values, in distinct territories.

Maybe Golding wants to say that the West and the communist East are behaving like twelve-year-olds, and that the battle is not really for supremacy but for a way of making a lasting peace.

Essays

Example Essay 1

How does Golding present violence in Lord of the Flies?

Plan

The key words here are "violence", "present" and "how".

Brainstorm the instances of violence- the killings of the sow and of the boy with the birthmark (in the fire in Chapter 2); the killing of Simon (mob violence); Jack's violence to Piggy, verbal ("shut up, Fatty") and physical (punching him, breaking his glasses); Roger killing Piggy, and throwing stones (at Henry, the twins, Ralph); his stick sharpened at both ends; his torture of the twins; the beating of Wilfred; Jack's violence to Ralph, in the last two chapters; the violence of the thunderstorm; the violence the Lord of the Flies threatens Simon with; the whole of Chapter 12.

Presented as- psychological sickness (Roger); personal, based on envy (Jack to Ralph) or hate (Jack to Ralph); irrational, mob psychology (killing Simon); a means of control (Jack on his tribe); a primitive drive (hunting); symbolic of breakdown of social order and cooperation- links to the allegorical dimension.

We have more than enough material here to write a 45-minute answer, so we have to be selective. Remember that the question does not ask us for a list of violent incidents; it asks us how Golding presents violence, not in part of the novel, but in the novel.

Start with our conclusion- there are different varieties of violence, but they all contribute to the overall meaning.

Then choose the most important (seven or so) examples, and write about them, concentrating on the words "how" and "present".

Possible answer-

The island from which the boys are rescued has become a violent place by the end of the novel, in contrast to the tropical holiday location it seemed when Ralph first swam in the lagoon in Chapter 1. Golding depicts different types of violence- for example, violent personal antagonism (directed by Jack towards Piggy and Ralph), the collective violence of the mob (when Simon is murdered), the psychopathic violence of the evil Roger, and the natural violence of fire in the forest.

There is much more violence in the second half of the narrative, which reflects the breaking down of the social framework which inhibited violence; it wears off. We should remember, too, that although Golding's novel is about boys on an island, it is also an allegory or literary device about how to keep the international peace in a nuclear world. In that context, Golding is asking us when we should press the button; when is violence justified or necessary, in order to deal with threats before (like a forest fire) they become out of control?

Some of the violence is symbolic. Jack's "hatred" of Piggy (and Ralph) runs all the way through the narrative, but Piggy's glasses are broken in Chapter 4, when Piggy confronts Jack over his failure to keep the fire alight; they become a central emblem of the transfer of power from Ralph to Jack, at the end of Chapter 10; and Jack still wears them, as a trophy, when the boys are rescued on the beach.

The breaking of the glasses dramatizes the conflict between the need for fire and the drive for hunting, which cannot be reconciled; that sustained clash also stands, symbolically, for the struggle for supremacy between the forces of civilised society and the forces of anarchy.

The murder of Simon at the end of Chapter 9 is a key point, because it indicates the final "breaking down" (as Ralph would put it) of the morals and conventions which keep the violence of Jack, Roger and the mob on some sort of leash.

Golding does not describe the killing in great detail; he does not need to, because he has already prepared for it, in the threatening scene in which the Lord of the Flies tells Simon that the boys- including Ralph and Piggy- will "do him" on the beach. The mob repeats the hunting chant five times; the last one adds the extra words "Do him in!".

Golding uses the reader's anticipation to make violence (or the threat of it) more appalling and powerful, in the same way, with Roger's "stick sharpened at both ends". When the twins tell Ralph that Roger has prepared one, for the final (man)hunt of Ralph, we know, long before Ralph realises it, that this means that Roger intends to put Ralph's severed head on the end of it. The potential for violence, pain, and the blurring between killing pigs and killing people, has been set up in the charade in Chapter 7, where Jack suggests that they could make the performance more realistic by using "a liitlun"- in fact, they use Simon.

Golding uses the character of Roger to convey the damage and impact of unrestrained violence. In Chapter 4, he throws stones to miss Henry because he is still influenced by the idea that society makes unprovoked violence illegal. At Castle Rock, he is liberated by the possibilities of irresponsible authority, when he hears that Wilfred is to be beaten, for no reason other than to inspire fear in the others. He throws stones close to the twins and Ralph in Chapter 11, before dropping the biggest stone so far on Piggy- not aiming to miss. He then takes over the torturing of the twins (who say that he is "a terror"), and we appreciate that he will be as sadistic to Ralph, if he catches him, as he was to the helpless sow in Chapter 8.

Rolling rocks is an interesting recurring aspect of violence. In Chapter 1, Ralph, Jack and Simon roll a large rock, and they feel exhilarated by the possibilities of adventure on the island, and their sense that it belongs to them. Balancing this, in Chapter 12, are the two rocks Jack and Roger roll, to force Ralph out into the open- the act is the same, but the motive and feeling behind it is completely different. Meanwhile, Roger, Jack and some others roll a rock at the end of Chapter 6, when they should be hunting the beast and re-lighting the fire (as Ralph tells them). This anticipates the rock Roger rolls on Piggy in Chapter 11; rocks become weapons of half-intended (Piggy) and intentional (Ralph) murder.

Pig-hunting is useful to Golding in setting mood and atmosphere. In the novel he wrote "Lord of the Flies" as an antidote to Ballantyne's "The Coral Island", the three boys hunt pigs without undue violence, and without bloodlust. Golding gives us the accidental encounter with a piglet in Chapter 1, where the boys cannot contemplate the change which the act of killing an animal will bring about in them.

Jack hunts alone at the start of Chapter 3; he throws his spear, but the pig escapes. Then he has his first successful hunt in Chapter 4, after inventing the technique of using paint as a disguise. We do not see this hunt- Jack recites it, and he now has the "knowledge" which comes with killing. The boar-hunt in Chapter 7 is the only hunt Ralph takes part in; he is almost seduced by the excitement it arouses in him, and this is important, because Golding wants to implicate all the boys- including Ralph and Piggy- in the murder of Simon, to support his point that nations lose their rational powers, and are gripped by a form of collective, irresistible madness, when they go to war.

The second hunt we see is the hunt of the sow, in Chapter 8; Golding conveys the terror of it by narrating it largely from a pig's point of view. After this, it is boys who are hunted- Simon, then Piggy, then Ralph. Simon is mistaken for the beast; Piggy is a boy whom Jack has always treated as though he were a pig; and Ralph is hunted because he is Jack's enemy. Chapter 12 sustains the violence of Jack's intentions very successfully, as we see how coldly and cleverly the hunt for Ralph is organised.

Rocks, pigs and glasses all contribute to the growing violence in the novel as power passes from the old, civilised, structured society (Ralph) to the anarchic, impulsive, trigger-happy world of Jack. Golding uses the threat of violence without constraint to raise, in the reader's mind, the allegorical problem of nuclear aggression in the post-War world of the 1950s. The boys are rescued, miraculously, because their story is an (updated) adventure yarn. In the real, "grown-up" world, maintaining peace may not be so easy.

Example Essay Two

Who, or what, is "the beast"? Explain its importance

Plan

To answer this question, we will need to do two things- first, define the beast and chart perceptions of it; second, evaluate what it brings to the meaning of the novel.

Material

The beast is discussed throughout; first, as snakes or creepers in the littluns' dreams/nightmares; later, as a ghost or a creature from the sea. Simon is mistaken for the beast, in the dark, in the camp, and when he comes out of the forest and is killed. The twins, Ralph, Jack and Roger all think the beast is the dead parachutist; reactions to that? How does Jack use the threat of the beast? The Lord of the Flies defines the beast to Simon. Is that the true definition? How do we know?

Conclusion

In the first half of the novel, the boys come to believe that there is a real, physical beast. In the second half, we come to see that "the beast" is the instinct to behave in a savage or unrestrained way. Link to psychology theories.

Possible Answer

Golding wrote "Lord of the Flies" partly to correct what he felt were the incorrect assumptions implicit in RM Ballantyne's "The Coral Island"- the innate superiority of British manners and leadership, the idea that savages (people of other races) can and should be controlled, and the premise that being shipwrecked on a tropical island is a recipe for a harmonious and happy life.

"The beast" first arises as "the snake-like thing" in the discussions in the assembly in Chapter 2- not the one in Chapter 1. One of the small boys claims he has seen it, that it is very big, and that it comes at night and wanted to eat him. Ralph tries to explain it away, both as a dream, and as a size of animal you would not find expect to find in a place like this island. Psychologists of Golding's time were interested in the idea that dreams are an outlet for repressed experience- a form of reality. Freud would say that the "id", the irrational part of us, where dark fears and savagery lurk in our subconscious, is "the beast".

Jack backs up Ralph's claims that there is no creature worthy of the title "the beast" (and he says that, if there were, he would hunt it and kill it); but, as Maurice points out in Chapter 5, no one can be certain that this is true- just because you haven't seen it doesn't disprove its existence. That assembly degenerates into a discussion about imagined sea-monsters and ghosts. On the island, in the dark, irrational fears exert a strong grip on the minds of small children, and no amount of reassurance can stop that. Golding uses the crying and wailing of Percival to dramatise the fear.

The dead parachutist drifts down on to the mountain during the night, and Sam and Eric are petrified when they see the body in the early morning at the start of Chapter 6. Their description of "the beast"- a winged, furry creature with claws and teeth, which followed them- scares everyone except Simon (who has a supernatural knowledge of the truth, both about the beast and about Ralph's escape or salvation). When Ralph, Jack and

Roger are equally terrified by the dead parachutist (they see it at night), Simon goes, by himself, and sets it free. It drifts out to sea, but only after Simon himself has been mistaken for the beast, as he staggers out of the forest with his blood-smeared face (from his fit-induced bleeding). Because Simon's explanation is drowned out, as he is torn and beaten to death in the thunderstorm, the myth of the beast lives on.

By the time the mob kills Simon- using Jack's hunting mantra to distract them from their lack of shelters at his end of the island- Jack is well on the way to taking the power to lead away from Ralph. He completes the process when he steals Piggy's glasses in Chapter 10. His hold over the boys arises from his capacity, as the hunter, to provide meat, and to protect them from the beast. He claims that the beast was not killed when Simon died, because it can disguise itself.

He has fallen for the mythology of the beast himself, or for the opportunity it gives him to raise his leadership credentials, when he leaves the sow's head as a peace offering for "the beast", and then when he uses the threat of its potential to attack as a way of keeping the boys in order, at Castle Rock. At first Ralph has allies in rationality, in Simon and Piggy, both of whom are sceptical about the beast. Once they are dead, though, Jack is the beast himself (supported in savagery by the sadist, Roger).

At the end of Chapter 8, the Lord of the Flies (a translation of "Beelzebub" from Hebrew, meaning "devil") tells Simon that it is the beast; that the beast cannot be hunted and killed; that it is "part of you"; and that, on the beach below, Simon will be the victim of the collective savagery of the beast, in the form of the mob violence of *all* the boys. Even the normally rational Piggy and Ralph will be attracted to "this demented but partly secure society".

Golding's point is that, as the rules and manners of civilised society wear off, there is less control over "the beast"- as law and order break down (because there is no "grown up" to enforce them) various forms of savagery, including murder, become common. Perhaps this is an attack on the idea (fostered by Britain's empire) that British boys behave best, as the naval officer presumes; left to their own devices, Golding's boys are not the morally upright citizens Ballantyne gave us in his characters (Ralph, Jack and Peterkin) even when they are taken out of British society.

For Golding, the British are capable of being just as savage as anyone else. The beast is the excitement of the mob, and it is universal in all cultures, whether we define them as civilised or primitive.

Psychologists in the 1940s and 1950s (Maslow, Ellis, Bowlby) were advancing theories about how children develop, and about the psychological needs of children, adolescents and adults. Where we have no family attachments (on a desert island) there is a strong drive to belong to a group, gang or "tribe". Where we have little shelter, and we feel our safety is fragile, we will not be capable of responsible citizenship; we will be more impulsive, less rational, more violent; we will hunt, and neglect the need for a signal fire, so that we can be rescued.

After the Second World War was ended by the atomic bomb dropped on Japan in 1945, the world became a more dangerous place. Pressing the nuclear button would be an impulsive act (of self-defence or aggression; it wouldn't matter which) which would wipe out whole nations without considering whether they were civilised or not. Like Ballantyne's boys, Golding's have spears and knives; but, behind Golding's novel, there lies the allegory of the political tensions of nationalism in a nuclear age.

Example Essay Three

"Ralph is out of his depth as a leader and he has only himself to blame for what goes wrong." To what extent do you agree with this opinion, and why?

<u>Key words:</u>

Opinion- agree- why

Plan

This question requires us to evaluate Ralph's personality and behaviour, as chief- he becomes increasingly distressed and isolated, as his allies (Piggy and Simon) are killed.

We have to make a judgment; could he have done better? Is Jack's grabbing of power inevitable, or has Ralph made it possible through some weakness of his own? If he has made mistakes, are they excusable? How do they affect the extent of our sympathy and support for him?

Our answer will need to be a balanced analysis of the demands which leadership makes, and how successful he is. Not all of the difficulties are of his own making.

Material

Ralph starts as an almost unanimous choice as leader. He finds a way to say what needs to be said. What weaknesses does he have? What does he do wrong (and what does he do right)? What does go wrong? And to what extent is it his fault, and to what extent are other people to blame?

Consider assemblies/the fire/ shelters and hunting/ Ralph's mental troubles/ Jack's opposition/ the way Ralph loses power/ Simon's murder/ Ralph's relationship with Piggy.

Possible Answer

When Ralph is chosen as chief at the first assembly, Golding tells us that the most obvious leader was Jack. Ralph is chosen, obscurely, because of his size, and attractive appearance; by virtue of his stillness; and the fact that he has blown the conch. He is appointed as leader not because he has shown a particular set of qualities but because he is the first boy to do anything which could be called leading- by blowing the conch.

He reassures the boys that they will be rescued, at the assembly in Chapter 2, and his success in raising their morale gives him a new authority. We read, at the start of that chapter, that "he found he could talk fluently and explain what he had to say". He grows into the job of being chief, and he is the only boy who understands- and keeps reminding the others- that they need to keep a signal fire burning.

He makes a mistake (from a leadership point of view) when he allows Jack to keep the choir under his command, and make them hunters. He does that because he wants to be friends with Jack, feels sorry for him and is eager to offer a consolation prize because he was not chosen to be leader. It is not Ralph's fault that Jack soon proves unhelpful, then mutinous, then antagonistic towards him; Jack soon comes to hate Ralph for no more complicated reason than because he wants to be chief (an ambition Piggy also has, though Piggy deals with his own disappointment in a more mature way).

Ralph proves unable to motivate the other boys to keep the fire going, and build enough shelters. Simon criticises him, quietly, in Chapter 3 ("You're chief. You tell 'em off") for not ensuring that the key tasks are done. While it is Jack's fault that the hunters allow the fire to go out (so that the opportunity of rescue is lost, in Chapter 4), because he has broken the promise he had made to the group in Chapter 2, a harsh critic would say that Ralph should have checked, to make sure that the task was done, rather than assume that other boys are reliable. He does criticise Piggy, in Chapter 2, when the consequence of Piggy's failure to count or keep the names of all the boys is that littluns may or may not have been burnt to death; but that was an impossible task.

Ralph does confront Jack when it is necessary, in order to protect Piggy, and make Jack responsible for his behaviour. He sets aside his own fear, to lead the way on the apparently dangerous hunt for the beast in the forest, but, at the top of the mountain, he is worn down by tiredness and puts himself in a position where Jack can accuse him of cowardice later. When he offers to support Piggy in the fatal mission to recover his glasses from Jack (in Chapter 11), Ralph does some of what a chief should do, but, for a long time- since the end of Chapter 5- he has doubted whether he should continue being leader. He finds it demoralising that the other boys do less than they need to do, and prefer playing and hunting to building shelters and keeping a good fire going. Beyond Chapter 1, he never manages to maintain a vision, or an overall agreement, or an organised effort to do the important things.

Ralph is a twelve-year-old who is thrust into the sort of responsibility which would normally be given only to an adult. Simon and Piggy support him; they are both horrified at the thought of what would happen if Jack were in charge instead (he'd have them out hunting all the time, at the expense of keeping the fire alive and thus keeping going their chance of rescue). But Simon is a poor speaker, and Piggy is an object of derision, so neither of them can give Ralph the help he needs.

Golding shows Ralph's ability to think clearly- his mental capacity, even- failing, as the novel goes on. This first arises in Chapter 5, where the assembly breaks down as law and order disintegrate. As the values of the civilised world weaken, so does Ralph's mental grip. In the next chapter, as he begins to doubt his previously strong belief that they will be rescued, and as Jack becomes troublesome, he is in a personal hell.

 At the end of Chapter 6, Ralph suffers his first mental malfunction. In Chapter 8, he confesses to Piggy that sometimes he no longer cares about the fire; then we are told that he experiences repeated mental anguish. To stop himself from complete breack down, he finds distraction and displacement in a tendency to daydream about being back in England, in a safe environment. This recurring misfiring is a result of overloading his mind with too much responsibility.

He tells the naval officer that two boys have been killed (Piggy and Simon) - forgetting the boy with the facial birthmark. The strain of what he defines, correctly, as Simon's murder, and losing Piggy, has left him friendless, hunted and isolated. In the final two chapters, the conflict between Jack and him is very much a moral one (evil versus good, wrong versus right, law and rescue versus hunting and breaking things up). The disintegration of Ralph's mind reflects the disintegration of his leadership; and that, in turn, mirrors the loss of order and the emergence, and temporary triumph, of evil, or the beast, in the savage character of Jack.

Tips for success

You'll have seen from the example essays that what counts is organising what you want to say (your plan!) then working steadily and succinctly through it. There is no need to over-write or to repeat a point for emphasis. Instead, think how you can develop and build each point you make – it is fine, for example, to give contrasting views. So Golding may be trying to explain what happens when civilised society breaks down, or he may be … Whatever your viewpoint if you *can back it up* with how a character or the plot develops, then this is fine.

Whatever your exam board is, look on its website, not just at questions on past papers, but at the mark schemes and the examiners' reports. Ask your English teacher to demystify the mark scheme and give you some tips.

And a pitfall to avoid

Don't fall into the trap of having a list of quotations you're determined to force into any essay. If you know the book- which you surely must by now!!- suitable short references will pop into your head (a two or three word quotation, for example, "an awesome stranger" to describe how Jack sees himself once he is painted as a savage, is sufficient).

Your number one focus is on answering the question in front of you.

Your number two focus is on answering the question.

So is focus number 3.

Answering the question means taking it apart and highlighting the key words (often that little word "how"); making a proper plan, which organises your material, gives you an argument and leads you to a clear and convincing conclusion; writing your essay from the plan; and stopping when you get to the end.

A proper plan means an essay that needs nothing added after its conclusion.

Please, please resist the temptation to start writing your essay straight away, even if many of those around you in the exam room do just that.

The exam allows you time to plan, and it is almost impossible to get a really good mark without a really good plan.

The test in the exam, then, is to choose relevant material, put it into an effective structure, and use your points to construct an argument, which you support by reference to the text, but not by copying out long quotations.

You should develop each of your points in one paragraph.

- Try to use fairly short sentences.
- When you have finished one point, go on to the next one.
- In your summary/concluding paragraph, you can say which point is the most important, and why.

Raise your grade tip:

Before you start writing your answer, put the points in your plan in order of importance. Write about them in order of importance, with the most important ones first.

That way, if you run out of time for that question, you'll only have left out your least important material.

Don't try to write too much, but *check-constantly- that what you are writing is actually answering the question in front of you.* If it isn't- leave it out.

Especially if you are taking your GCSE this summer, I wish you every success.

Gavin Smithers is a private tutor, covering Broadway, Chipping Campden and the North Cotswolds. He has an English degree from Oxford University, and a passion for helping others to discover the joy and satisfaction of great literature.

Gavin's Guides are short books packed with insight. Their key aim is to help you raise your grade!

The series is available as e-book and paperback. Details and reviews of the series are on Gavin Smithers' Amazon page.

Titles include:

> *Understanding J.B. Priestley's An Inspector Calls*
> *Understanding Charles Dickens' Great Expectations*
> *Understanding John Steinbeck's Of Mice and Men*
> *Understanding Emily Dickinson's Set Poems*
> *Understanding Edward Thomas' Set Poems*
> *Understanding Andrew Marvell's Cromwell & Eulogy Poems*

And finally.........if there's anything you're still not sure about, and if your teacher can't help, please contact the author- grnsmithers@hotmail.co.uk

9789366R00072

Printed in Great Britain
by Amazon.co.uk, Ltd.,
Marston Gate.